Activity Book A

VISIONS

Language · Literature · Content

Mary Lou McCloskey

Lydia Stack

THOMSON

™

HEINLE

Australia ◇ Canada ◇ Mexico ◇ Singapore ◇ United Kingdom ◇ United States

VISIONS ACTIVITY BOOK A
Mary Lou McCloskey and Lydia Stack

Publisher: *Phyllis Dobbins*
Director of Development: *Anita Raducanu*
Developmental Editor: *Tania Maundrell-Brown*
Associate Developmental Editor: *Yeny Kim*
Associate Developmental Editor: *Kasia Zagorski*
Editorial Assistant: *Audra Longert*
Production Supervisor: *Mike Burggren*
Marketing Manager: *Jim McDonough*
Manufacturing Manager: *Marcia Locke*
Director, ELL Training and Development: *Evelyn Nelson*
Photography Manager: *Sheri Blaney*
Development: *Proof Positive/Farrowlyne Associates, Inc.; Quest Language Systems, LLC*
Design and Production: *Proof Positive/Farrowlyne Associates, Inc.*
Cover Designer: *Studio Montage*
Printer: *Patterson Printing*

Cover Image: *© Danny Lehman/Index Stock Imagery*

Printed in the United States of America.
7 8 9 10   08   07   06

For more information, contact Heinle, 25 Thomson Place, Boston, Massachusetts 02210 USA, or you can visit our Internet site at http://www.heinle.com

For permission to use material from this text or product contact us:
Tel   1-800-730-2214
Fax   1-800-730-2215
Web www.thomsonrights.com

ISBN: 0-8384-5284-1

Contents

Build Vocabulary

Use with student text page 3.

Define and Alphabetize Words

Define Words

A. ➤ Match the underlined word in each sentence to its definition. Read the sentences carefully. They will help you understand the words.

Word in a Sentence

1. __*a*__ He answered the difficult question. Then he <u>smirked</u>.

2. _____ The <u>mesquite wood</u> began to burn.

3. _____ My aunt is good at <u>comforting</u> people when they feel bad.

4. _____ My mother baked and <u>decorated</u> the cake.

5. _____ My father put the chicken and vegetables on the <u>barbecue</u>.

Definition

a. smiled in a way that showed you felt smarter or better than someone else

b. making someone feel better

c. a type of wood

d. made beautiful

e. a place for cooking food outdoors

Identify Words in Alphabetical Order

The letters of the alphabet are in alphabetical order.

ABCDEFGHIJKLMNOPQRSTUVWXYZ

The words in a dictionary are in alphabetical order. This makes words easy to find. The following words from the reading selection are in alphabetical order:

barbecue, **c**omforting, **t**eenagers

B. ➤ Put these letters in alphabetical order. The first one has been done for you.

1. T G V ___*G T V*___

2. Z A B _____

3. P C L _____

4. B O L _____

C. ➤ Put a check mark (✓) next to the groups of words that are in alphabetical order.

1. _____ smirking, rabbit ears, teenagers

2. _____ comforting, designed, underneath

3. _____ ripples, decorate, encouraging

Writing: Spelling

Use with student text page 10.

Spell Homophones

Some English words are pronounced the same even though they have different spellings and meanings. These words are called **homophones.**
Look at the spellings and definitions of the homophones in the chart.

Homophones	Meanings
meat	food from the muscle of animals
meet	plan to see someone
sum	the total amount of something
some	an unknown amount

Homophones	Meanings
one	a single person or thing
won	the past tense of *win*
him	possessive form of *he*
hymn	a religious song

A. ➤ Underline the correct word in each sentence. The first one has been done for you.

1. I will (meat/<u>meet</u>) you at the store after school.

2. Miguel encouraged (him/hymn) to try out for the play.

3. There are (sum/some) benches under the tree.

4. She wanted to take (won/one) last picture of her family.

B. ➤ Underline the word that is a homonym for the word in darker type.

1. **flour:**   floor   <u>flower</u>   four

2. **great:**   grate   gate   gear

3. **there**   that   their   tear

4. **would**   will   want   wood

5. **stairs**   start   stares   stars

Elements of Literature

Use with student text page 11.

Recognize First-Person Point of View

A **narrator** is the person telling a story. A narrator uses the **first-person point of view** when he or she is a character in the story.

The narrator uses the pronouns *I, me, mine, we, us,* and *ours* and the adjectives *my* and *our* to tell a story in the first-person point of view.

A. ➤ Read these sentences. Write "First" if a sentence is in the first-person point of view. Write "X" if it is not in the first-person point of view.

_____ **1.** When spring comes, Hector begins to think about soccer. He loves soccer.

_____ **2.** My sister, Graciela, and I love to play soccer.

_____ **3.** We often play for hours.

B. ➤ Complete the story with the first-person pronouns and adjectives from the box.

I	me	my
we	us	our

When spring comes, _____*I*_____ begin to think about soccer. Soccer is

_____ favorite sport. _____ sister, Graciela, and

_____ love to play. _____ often play for hours.

_____ both dream of becoming professional soccer players.

_____ hope _____ dream will come true.

The World Cup is in _____ city this year. Yesterday,

_____ sister surprised _____. She said, "We have tickets to

the World Cup!" _____ grandpa and grandma bought the tickets for

_____. _____ can't wait to see _____

favorite teams play.

Word Study

Use with student text page 12.

Understand and Define Compound Words

A **compound word** is a word made up of two smaller words.

book + store → bookstore

door + bell → doorbell

Can you think of another compound word that is made with one of the smaller words above? *Doorknob* and *bookcase* are two other compound words.

If you know the meaning of the smaller words, you can often figure out the meaning of compound words. For example, if you know what *book* and *store* mean, you will know that *bookstore* means "a store where you buy books."

A. ➤ Underline the compound words in the paragraph. The first one has been done for you.

Today was my <u>birthday</u>. I had a nice party. Most of my girlfriends were there. My grandfather and grandmother were there, too. I got some nice gifts. One of them was a nice backpack. Another gift was a cotton sundress. The party was great except the headache I got that evening.

B. ➤ Fill in the chart. Use the compound words in the paragraph.

Compound Word	Word	Word	Meaning
birthday	birth	day	the day on which a person is born
			friends that are girls
			a parent's father
			a parent's mother
			a bag carried on one's back
			a dress worn in warm weather
			a pain in the head

Grammar Focus

Use the Present Continuous Tense Verbs

Use with student text page 12.

A **verb** is a word that shows action. Verbs in the **present continuous tense** tell about an action that is happening now.

Present Continuous Tense			
Subject	Present Tense of *Be*	Base Verb + *-ing*	Sentence
I	am	go + *-ing*	I am going home.
You, We, They	are		We are going home.
He, She, It	is		She is going home.

Here are some spelling rules for adding *-ing* to verbs:
1. If a verb is one syllable and ends in a vowel plus one consonant (sw**im**, s**it**), double the consonant and add *-ing* (swi**mm**ing, si**tt**ing).
2. If a verb ends in a consonant + *e* (los**e**, liv**e**), drop the *e* and add *-ing* (losing, living).
3. For most verbs that end in an *i* + *e* (**die**, **lie**), change the *e* to a *y* and add *-ing* (dying, lying).
4. Just add *-ing* to most other verbs (walking, writing).

enjoy	tie	cry	feed
put	make	save	cook

➤ Underline the correct form of *be* to form present continuous sentences. Then complete each sentence with a verb from the box and add *-ing*.

1. My Dad (am/<u>is</u>/are) _____*cooking*_____ dinner tonight.

2. My grandmother (am/is/are) _____ cookies.

3. You (am/is/are) _____ all of your money for a new bike.

4. I (am/is/are) _____ the baby.

5. The baby (am/is/are) _____ now.

6. I (am/is/are) _____ my shoes.

7. They (am/is/are) _____ the food away.

8. We (am/is/are) _____ our visit with you.

Grammar Focus

Use with student text page 12.

Use Present Continuous Tense Questions, Negatives, and Contractions

Questions

To form a present continuous tense question, put the form of *be* before the subject.

Present Continuous Tense Questions		
Form of *Be*	Subject	Verb + *-ing*
Am	I	
Are	you, we, they	working?
Is	he, she, it	

A. ➤ Rewrite the statements as questions. The first one has been done for you.

1. I am thinking. _____*Are you thinking?*_____

2. They are shoveling the walk. _____

3. She is cooking. _____

Negatives and Contractions

To make a present continuous negative statement, add *not* to *am, are,* or *is*.

I am <u>not</u> going.

Contractions are formed by joining two words together. Letters are dropped and replaced with an apostrophe (').

You <u>aren't</u> going. (are not → aren't)   He <u>isn't</u> going. (is not → isn't)

Note: *Am not* does not have a contracted form.

B. ➤ Rewrite the present continuous sentences in the negative form. Then rewrite them in the negative form with contractions. The first one has been done for you.

1. You are bringing your dog with you.

   You are not bringing your dog with you. You aren't bringing your dog with you.

2. We are enjoying our vacation.

   _____

Student Handbook

From Reading to Writing

Use with student text page 13.

Edit a Personal Narrative

➤ Use the checklist to edit the paragraphs you wrote in Chapter 1.

Editing Checklist for a Personal Narrative

_____ **1.** I drew a picture of a family celebration or a party. I put myself in the picture.

_____ **2.** I wrote a personal narrative about the picture

_____ **3.** I wrote in the first-person point of view. I used the words *I, me, mine, my, we, us, ours,* or *our* to show that I am the narrator.

_____ **4.** I used present continuous tense verbs.

_____ **5.** I wrote one or two paragraphs.

Across Content Areas

Use with student text page 13.

Follow How-To Steps

Many books have instructions. These instructions tell you how to make something.

What You Need to Make a Piñata:

- round balloon
- flour
- tempera paints
- scissors
- old newspapers
- water
- string
- candy

What You Do:

1. Blow up a large balloon, but not too tightly.

2. Make a paste (mixture) by stirring together flour and water.

3. Cut the newspapers into strips.

4. Dip the newspaper strips into the flour and water paste. Cover the balloon with the strips.

5. Let dry overnight.

6. Repeat this process for four more days. Then let the balloon dry.

7. On the fifth day, paint the balloon with a design.

8. Let the paint dry on the balloon. Cut a hole at the top of it. Then fill it with candy.

9. Make holes on opposite sides. Put a string through the holes.

10. Tie the piñata to a pole. Then enjoy your piñata at a party or gathering.

➤ Answer the questions. Use the instructions.

1. What is the first step in making a piñata?

   _____

2. What might happen if you do not follow Step 1 exactly?

   _____

3. For which step would you use scissors? _____

4. What do you put into the piñata? _____

5. How many days does it take to complete the piñata? _____

VISIONS A Activity Book · Copyright © Heinle

Name _____ Date _____

Build Vocabulary

Use with student text page 15.

Use Definitions and Alphabetize Words

Word and Definition	
darted moved very quickly	**dark** with little or no light
lumbered ran or walked in a heavy way	**gleaming** shining brightly
soared flew through the air easily	**forest** an area of land with many trees
stirred moved slightly	**prairie** a large area with tall grasses
bright very light or clear	**mountains** tall pieces of land higher than hills

Use Definitions

A. ➤ Complete the story. Use the words in the box.

The sun was very ___*bright*___. The water on the grass was
1
_____ in the sunlight. A flock of birds _____ in the blue
2   3
sky. A monkey was waking from a nap. It _____, but was too sleepy to
4
climb down from the large tree branch.

I was in a tree house. Below me, I could see many elephants. They
_____ on their heavy feet through the _____, which had
5   6
many different trees. Beyond the trees, I could see the _____. It was a sea
7
of grass. There were some deer playing. They _____ back and forth, as
8
though they were playing tag.

I could see snow-covered _____. They seemed to reach up to the sky.
9
It was beginning to get _____. I decided to go home.
10

Alphabetize Words

When the first letters of a set of words are the same, you have to look at the second
letter in words to put them in alphabetical order.

small   **so**und   **st**ill

B. ➤ Write each set of words in alphabetical order.

1. flung, forest, first   ___*first, flung, forest*___

2. grew, galloped, glared   _____

Writing: Spelling

Use with student text page 22.

Spell Words with the Vowels *ea* and *ee*

Many English words have the vowels *ea* and *ee*. Two vowels placed together in a word that make one sound are called a **vowel digraph.**

Read these words with *ea* and *ee* aloud: *meat, meet*. Both words are pronounced with a long *e* as in *see*.

Look at the chart. It shows some words that are pronounced with a long *e* sound and have the vowels *ea* and *ee*.

Words with *ea*	Words with *ee*
dream	sweet
beat (rhythm)	beet (a vegetable)
real	feel
beam (shine)	feet

When you **edit** your writing, you check it for spelling, grammar, and punctuation mistakes. You also check your work to be sure sentences make sense.

➤ Edit these sentences. Rewrite the sentences by correcting the spellings of the words that should have the letters *ea* or *ee*.

1. Last night, I had a very sweat dreem.

Last night, I had a very sweet dream.

2. In the dreem, I was a great dancer with very skilled feat!

_____

3. I was a dancer, and I could feel the music as I moved to each beet.

_____

4. The audience clapped and clapped as I beemed like a star from the stage.

_____

5. I finally woke up. My dreem seamed so real.

_____

VISIONS A Activity Book • Copyright © Heinle

Elements of Literature

Analyze the Author's Purpose

Use with student text page 23.

A writer's reason for writing a text is called the **author's purpose.** Look at the list of purposes for writing.

Author's Purpose
to entertain to amuse or provide fun
to inform to give information about a topic
to persuade to lead readers to believe or do something
to express an opinion to tell readers the author's thoughts and feelings about a topic

---

Writing often has more than one purpose. For example, an article about sports might entertain and inform.

➤ Fill in the chart. Write the author's purpose in the second column.

Text	Author's Purpose
1. The unemployment rate went up in January. This was the third straight month that the jobless rate increased.	inform
2. You should vote for Valerie Stillman. If she is elected, she will make sure everyone has a job.	
3. Did you know that whales are not fish? They are mammals that spend their entire lives in the sea. Whales are related to dolphins and porpoises.	
4. I think that Brazil will win the World Cup this year. The team always has strong soccer players. Brazil has won many World Cups in past years.	
5. I went fishing the other day. The only thing that I caught was a bad cold and someone's old shoes.	

Word Study

Use with student text page 24.

Use a Synonym Finder

Synonyms are words that have similar meanings. For example, the verb *run* has many synonyms. Some of them are *sprint, jog, scuttle, scamper, dart,* and *dash.*

Writers often use synonyms to make their writing more vivid and interesting.

You can use a **synonym finder** to locate synonyms for words. A synonym finder lists words in alphabetical order.

➤ Read these entries from a synonym finder. Then rewrite each sentence using a word from the synonym finder.

> **cry:** shriek, holler, bay, wail, scream
> **run:** scuttle, bound, dash, bustle, scurry, dart, scamper, gallop
> **quiet:** calm, still, tranquil, motionless

1. The coyote <u>howled</u> at the moon.

   The coyote cried at the moon.
   _____

2. The night was <u>quiet</u>.

   _____

   _____

3. The young boys <u>bounded</u> into the room.

   _____

   _____

4. The wind was <u>calm</u>.

   _____

   _____

Grammar Focus

Use with student text page 24.

Identify Subjects and Verbs in Sentences

A complete sentence has a subject and a verb. The **subject** of a sentence is *who* or *what* the sentence is about. The **verb** shows the action of the sentence. A subject *does* the action of the verb.

   Subject   Verb
Coyotes hunt for food during the night.

A sentence can have more than one subject or verb.

  Subject   Subject   Verb   Verb
Ramona and Gabriela walked downtown and met for lunch.

A. ➤ Underline the subject in each sentence.

1. <u>Coyote</u> blinked his eyes in the darkness.

2. His growl made forests and grass prairies.

3. I have no one to run with.

4. With his sharp claws, Coyote dug in the bank and made heaps of clay.

5. Andrew Matthews lives in Great Britain.

B. ➤ Underline the verb in each sentence. The first one has been done for you.

1. Coyote <u>ran</u> through the world he had made.

2. He found a river with a high bank.

3. His growl made forests and grassy plains.

4. Coyote took colors to the five corners of the Earth and then he waited.

5. The colors grew into the sky and bent together in the first rainbow.

Grammar Focus

Use with student text page 24.

Use Subjects and Verbs in Sentences

A. ➤ Unscramble the sentence parts to make correct sentences.

1. the dog/to the park./I walked

    I walked the dog to the park.

2. scampered/He/up the hill.

    _____

3. Heather/walked to the store./and Jane

    _____

4. cooked/some delicious vegetables./My father

    _____

5. The two girls/from Chicago/danced and sang.

    _____

B. ➤ Write sentences using these pairs of subjects and verbs. Use a capital (large) letter to start each sentence. Use a period (.) to end it.

1. Coyote/howled

    The coyote howled at the moon.

2. boys/played

    _____

3. baseball team/won

    _____

4. Jesse, Adrian, and Jill/wanted

    _____

5. My brother and I/like

    _____

Student
Handbook

From Reading to Writing

Use with student text page 25.

Edit a Narrative

➤ Use the checklist to edit the narrative you wrote in Chapter 2.

Editing Checklist for a Narrative

Title of narrative: _____

_____ 1. I used my imagination to develop an animal character that creates something in nature.

_____ 2. I gave my story a title.

_____ 3. I wrote my story in one or two paragraphs.

_____ 4. I gave my story a beginning, a middle, and an end.

_____ 5. I chose my words carefully to be sure that my story makes sense.

_____ 6. I capitalized and punctuated my story correctly to strengthen its meaning.

Across Content Areas

Use with student text page 25.

Take Notes

Read the article about coyotes. Think about the question: How do coyotes communicate?

Coyotes

The coyote is an animal that is similar to a medium-sized dog. Coyotes are common in the western part of the United States. They often live in desert areas. Many people connect a coyote's nighttime howls to their images of the desert. Read more about the sounds coyotes make to communicate with each another.

A Coyote's Howl

In certain places, you can hear coyotes howling at night. A howl sounds like a loud cry. Coyotes howl to let other coyotes know where they are. They may also do this to tell other coyotes to stay away from their area of land.

Barking Dog

Coyotes bark just like other dogs do. The scientific name for coyotes actually means *barking dog*. Coyotes bark at people or animals when they are protecting their home or food. It is their way of saying, "Stay away or I will attack."

Playful Yelping

A yelp is a sharp, quick cry. Baby coyotes often yelp when they are playing. Coyotes also yelp to communicate disapproval (dislike).

Quiet Huffing

A coyote's huff is a breathy, soft sound. Coyotes sometimes huff to quietly call their young.

➤ Fill in the note card.
   Use the article.

How do coyotes communicate?
Howling:
Barking:
Yelping:
Huffing:

Build Vocabulary

Use with student text page 27.

Use Synonyms and Guide Words

Synonyms are words that have similar meanings. *Big* and *large* are synonyms.

Word and Definition

gobbled ate in a quick and hungry way
stuffed having eaten too much
remember think of something from the past
dish something used to serve and hold food
wonderful very good; very pleasing
hurry rush; go quickly
feast a large meal
piece part of something

A. ➤ Write a synonym for each underlined word. Use the words in the box.

1. I <u>recall</u> many happy Thanksgivings. *remember* _____

2. One Thanksgiving we were running late. "We had better <u>rush</u> over to Grandma's house," my mother said. _____

3. We arrived there just in time for the <u>large meal</u>. _____

4. I had a large <u>portion</u> of turkey. _____

5. I <u>quickly</u> ate my whole <u>plate</u> of food. _____

6. I was really <u>full</u> after dinner. All of the food was <u>great</u>. _____

Use Guide Words

Guide words are the words at the top of each dictionary page. The first guide word is the first word listed on that dictionary page. The second guide word is the last word listed on that page.

B. ➤ Read the guide words. Underline the word in each group that would be listed between the guide words on a dictionary page.

Guide Words	**Words**
1. **tunic / turn**	turnip, <u>turkey</u>, take
2. **faze / feature**	fixture, face, feast
3. **woe / woods**	wash, would, wonderful
4. **badge / balance**	bake, balloon, baseball

Writing: Capitalization

Use with student text page 38.

Capitalize Months, Days, Calendar Events, Countries, and People

We always capitalize the first word in a sentence. Read some other capitalization rules in the chart:

Always Capitalize	Examples
days of the week	Monday
months of the year	January
calendar events	Christmas
groups of people	Mexicans
individuals	Julio
countries	Vietnam

➤ Edit these sentences. Rewrite the sentences by correcting the capitalization errors. The first one has been done for you.

1. Each year in november, we like to celebrate thanksgiving.
   Each year in November, we like to celebrate Thanksgiving.

2. the pilgrims learned many new things.
   _____

3. Uncle bob carves the turkey better than anyone in our family.
   _____

4. After Thanksgiving, my favorite holiday is christmas.
   _____

5. Christmas is celebrated in december every year.
   _____

6. I think that new year's day falls on tuesday this year.
   _____

7. The native americans grew corn and squash for the feast.
   _____

8. aunt betty and my cousins will be at my birthday party.
   _____

9. The pilgrims were from england.
   _____

10. Cousins laura and matt came to our house.
   _____

VISIONS A Activity Book • Copyright © Heinle

Elements of Literature

Use with student text page 39.

Identify and Use Rhyme

Many poems use words that **rhyme.** Words that rhyme have the same ending sound. For example, *cat* and *bat* rhyme. *Sneak* and *peak* rhyme.

The poem "Thanksgiving" has a rhyme scheme, a plan for using words that rhyme. Look at these lines from "Thanksgiving":

We finally arrive at a little past <u>four</u>—

The whole family's waving at Grandma's front <u>door.</u>

In "Thanksgiving," the rhyme scheme is for the last words in each line of a stanza to rhyme. *Four* rhymes with *door.*

A. ➤ Underline the words that rhyme in this poem.

My Favorite Book

I love to hide with my favorite book.

Where no one can find me or easily look.

I'm in faraway lands of dragons and kings

And knights who fight the most terrible things.

When the day's reading is done, I return home.

But tomorrow again with my book I will roam.

B. ➤ Underline the rhyming word for each pair of lines.

1. I once had a cat named Sally.

She lived in a box by the (<u>alley</u>/house/garage).

2. The two little boys had a big, orange ball

That they played with until they heard Mother's (yell/cry/call).

3. Tomas had a big dog named Pete.

A lazy, old dog who just wanted to (eat/dig/sleep).

4. Out of nowhere appeared the little, gray mouse.

We watched it and wondered how it entered the (room/house/kitchen).

5. Yesterday, I caught a large, flopping fish.

I dragged it to shore for the evening's main (meal/dinner/dish).

Word Study

Use with student text page 40.

Use the Suffixes *-ful* and *-less*

A **suffix** is a group of letters added to the end of a word. A suffix changes the meaning of the word.

➤ Read the chart to learn about the suffixes *-ful* and *-less.*

Suffix	Suffix Meaning	Word	Word Meaning	Word in Context
-ful	full of	thoughtful	full of thought	She always thinks about other people. She is thoughtful.
-less	without	thoughtless	without thought	He only thinks about himself. He is thoughtless.

➤ Rewrite the sentences by replacing the underlined words with a word that has the suffix *-ful* or *-less.* The first one has been done for you.

1. She was <u>full of cheer</u> when she received the present.

   She was cheerful when she received the present.

2. After looking all morning, she felt <u>without hope</u> about finding her dog.

   _____

3. Rita was <u>full of thanks</u> to have known her teacher.

   _____

4. I want to travel in space. I think the experience would be <u>full of wonder</u>.

   _____

5. For days, we traveled on a road that seemed <u>without end</u>.

   _____

6. The cruel queen was <u>without heart</u>.

   _____

7. I need a vacation that is <u>full of peace</u>.

   _____

Grammar Focus

Use with student text page 40.

Use Subject Pronouns

Subject pronouns can be used in place of nouns that are subjects.

<u>Martina</u> walked to school. <u>Martina</u> was late.

Martina can be replaced by the subject pronoun *she* in the second sentence.

<u>Martina</u> walked to school. <u>She</u> was late.

Subject Pronouns			
	First Person	**Second Person**	**Third Person**
SINGULAR	I	you	he, she, it
PLURAL	we	you	they

➤ **A.** Rewrite the second sentence of each pair by replacing the underlined noun with a subject pronoun. The first one has been done for you.

1. The people were thankful for the food they had grown. <u>The people</u> held a great feast with plenty to eat.

   They held a great feast with plenty to eat.

2. Baby Emma is crying. <u>Baby Emma</u> must be hungry.

   _____

3. Uncle Bob carves the turkey. <u>Uncle Bob</u> does it well.

   _____

4. The squirrel ran across the yard. <u>The squirrel</u> seemed to be busy.

   _____

➤ **B.** Edit these sentences. Rewrite the sentences by correcting the subject pronouns.

1. Yesterday, my friends came over. Them wanted to go out.

   Yesterday, my friends came over. They wanted to go out.

2. Anna, James, and me went to a movie. He was a comedy.

   _____

3. Anna laughed through the movie. It thought it was the funniest story.

   _____

4. James did not laugh much through the movie. "It is not that funny," him said.

   _____

Grammar Focus

Use with student text page 40.

Understand and Use Pronoun Referents

A **pronoun referent** is the noun that a pronoun replaces. In the following sentences, the pronoun referent is the subject *Pilgrims.* The pronoun that replaces *Pilgrims* is *they.*

The *Pilgrims* traveled a great distance to get to the Americas. *They* must have been very tired after the trip.

➤ **A.** Underline the pronoun in the second sentence of each pair. Then underline with two lines the pronoun referent in the first sentence.

1. On Thanksgiving, <u>people</u> give thanks for the good things in their lives. <u>They</u> eat a big meal with family members and friends.

2. Father made bread made from corn. Then he baked a dessert.

3. Antonio, Cattia, and Sonia helped clean the house. Then they took a nap.

4. Thanksgiving always falls on a Thursday. It falls on the fourth Thursday of November.

5. My sister is older than I am. She is fourteen, and I am twelve.

➤ **B.** Write sentences that have the following pronoun referents and pronouns.

1. Mary/she

_____

_____

2. Fernando/he

_____

_____

3. the dog/it

_____

_____

Student
Handbook

VISIONS A Activity Book • Copyright © Heinle

From Reading to Writing

Use with student text page 41.

Edit a Narrative

➤ Use the checklist to edit the narrative you wrote in Chapter 3.

Editing Checklist for a Narrative

Title of narrative: _____

_____ 1. I based my narrative on the questions that I asked myself before writing. These questions were:

_____What is the important holiday?

_____When do we celebrate it?

_____Why do we celebrate it?

_____How do we prepare for the holiday?

_____How do we celebrate the holiday?

_____ 2. I used the writing model on page 41 of my textbook.

_____ 3. I wrote a title for my narrative.

_____ 4. I used singular and plural nouns and pronouns correctly to show people, places, and things.

_____ 5. I used a resource such as a dictionary to correctly spell words.

Across Content Areas

Use with student text page 41.

Preview Text

It is often helpful to preview a text before you read it.

Steps for Previewing

1. Look through the selection you will read. Look at photographs, charts, graphs, and other illustrations. Ask yourself: What do these visuals tell me about the selection?

2. Look at the main headings in the text. They give clues about important ideas.

3. Look at any boldfaced words (words in dark type). Ask yourself: How many of these words do I already know? How do they relate to my experiences?

4. Use a **KWL chart** to help you organize your reading. The **K** stands for what you already **know** about a topic. The **W** stands for what you **want** to learn. The **L** stands for what you **learned** after you read a text.

➤ Fill in the KWL chart to preview the next reading selection in your book. Fill in the K and W columns of the chart. After you read the selection, fill in the L column.

Know / Want to Know / Learned Chart		
K	**W**	**L**

Name _____ Date _____

Build Vocabulary

Use with student text page 43.

Use Dictionary Entries

A **dictionary entry** shows information about a word's meaning and pronunciation. Some dictionaries tell which language a word came from (its origin).

All dictionary entries have **headwords** and definitions. Headwords are usually boldfaced (in dark type). The definitions tell the meanings of the words. Many dictionary entries show more than one meaning for a word.

headword ——————	**play** /plā/ *verb* **1** to have fun, amuse ——— *definition 1* oneself: *Children played with a ball on the beach.* **2** to participate in a sport or ——— *definition 2* game: *She plays tennis, and he plays cards.* **3** to compete against in sport or ——— *definition 3* game: *Our basketball team played against the state champions.* **4** to ——— *definition 4* perform on a musical instrument: *She played the violin.* [Old English *plega*] ——— *word origin*

➤ Decide which definition for *play* fits each sentence. Write the number of the correct definition in the space. The first one has been done for you.

1. ____4____ I play the guitar in a band.

2. _____ I wanted to play volleyball at the beach, but it was too hot.

3. _____ My favorite baseball team will play in the World Series.

4. _____ My little brother kept asking me to play with him.

Writing: Spelling

Use with student text page 50.

Change the Spelling of Words Ending in *e*

When a word ends in *e*, the spelling often changes when an ending is added to it. When adding endings to words that end in *e*, follow these rules:

Rule for Words Ending in a Consonant + *e*	Example
When an ending for a word ending in e begins with a vowel, drop the e before adding the ending.	give + ing = giving care + ed = cared sense + ible = sensible
When an ending for a word ending in e begins with a consonant, keep the e when adding the ending.	hope + ful = hopeful wide + ly = widely love + ly = lovely

➤ Edit these sentences. Rewrite the sentences to correct the spelling errors. The first one has been done for you.

1. He was haveing a good time.

   He was having a good time. _____

2. She is weaveing a rug.

   _____

3. He is probabley going to be late for dinner.

   _____

4. He held the papers loosly in his hands.

   _____

5. The baby is very lovly in her new dress.

   _____

6. She is carefully arrangeing the flowers.

   _____

7. He is a very carless person.

   _____

VISIONS A Activity Book • Copyright © Heinle

Name _____ Date _____

Elements of Literature

Use with student text page 51.

Write Instructions

Instructions tell you how to do something. Many instructions are written in **sequence,** or in order of steps. They tell what to do first, what to do next, and so on.

Read these instructions for making sun iced tea.

Sun Iced Tea

A fun thing to do on a hot, sunny day is to make sun iced tea. Begin in the morning and be sure it will be hot and sunny out all day.

Find a sturdy glass jar with a lid. Fill the jar with water. Place tea bags of your favorite flavor in the water. Put the lid on the jar. Put the jar outside in direct sunlight. Leave the jar outside all day. When the sun starts going down, bring the jar inside. Remove the tea bags and add sugar and ice. Your sun iced tea is ready to enjoy!

➤ Fill in the flowchart. Use the steps in the recipe.

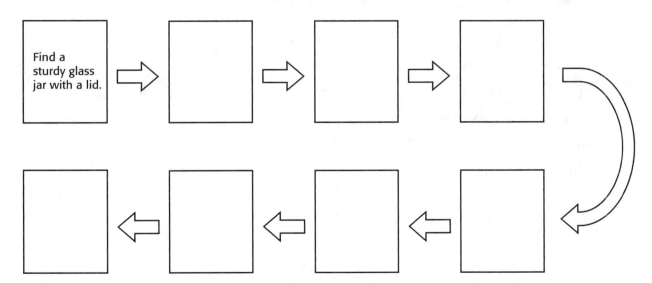

Word Study

Use with student text page 52.

Use Root Words and the Suffixes -ish and -like

A **root word** is a word or part of a word that can be used to make other words.

A **suffix** is a group of letters that is added to the end of a word. A suffix changes the meaning of the word. The suffix -*like* means "like something." The suffix -*ish* means "like something" or "having to do with."

The word *child* can be a root word. You can make other words from *child* by adding suffixes to the end of the word. The suffixes -*ish* and -*like* can both be added to *child*. *Childish* and *childlike* both mean "like a child."

Root Word	Root Word + *like*	Root Word	Root Word + *ish*
wolf	wolflike	England	English
business	businesslike	style	stylish
cat	catlike	fever	feverish

➤ Complete each sentence with one of the words in the chart.

1. The medium-sized dog had a bushy tail and had a ___wolflike___ face.

2. She had a sore throat. She said she also felt _____.

3. If you have a job interview, you should wear _____ clothing.

4. The dancer was known for his graceful and _____ movements.

5. Emma was born in London, England. She is _____.

6. Maura likes to wear nice clothing. She always looks _____.

Grammar Focus

Use with student text page 52.

Use the Verb *To Be* with Complements

A **complement** describes or renames the subject of a sentence. The complement is underlined in the sentence below. It describes *my mother,* the subject in the sentence.

My mother is a hardworking woman.

Complements often follow a form of the verb *to be*. The three verbs shown in the chart are examples of the verb *to be*.

Subject	Form of the Verb *To Be*	Complement (a noun, a pronoun, or an adjective)
I	am	thirsty.
You, We, They, The girls, The boys	are	
He, She, It, Manuel, Theresa	is	

➤ **A.** Underline the correct form of the verb *to be*. Circle the complement.

1. I (am/are/is) 13 years old.

2. When spring comes, we (am/are/is) (happy) because it is warm.

3. Two of my sisters (am/are/is) good carpet weavers.

4. During holidays, we (am/are/is) usually busy.

5. She (am/are/is) very talented.

➤ **B.** Write three sentences. Use the subjects and *be* verbs indicated. Choose complements for the sentences. Circle the complements.

1. (subject: I/verb: am)

_____

2. (subject: the tree/verb: is)

_____

3. (subject: my friends/verb: are)

_____

Name _____ Date _____

Grammar Focus

Use with student text page 52.

Use the Verb *To Be* with Complements: Question, Negative, and Contracted Forms

To form a question with a subject, a *to be* verb, and a complement, put the *to be* verb before the subject. Then add a question mark (?).

She is nice.

Is she nice?

➤ **A.** Rewrite the statements as questions.

1. They are always late. ___*Are they always late?*_____

2. Clarissa is her best friend. _____

3. You are in Turkey. _____

4. It is blue and green. _____

5. Thalia and Sean are neighbors. _____

To be verbs have negative forms. Negative forms of *to be* verbs have the word *not* after them. You can also make contractions of *to be* verbs + *not*.

Full Forms	Contractions
I <u>am not</u> hungry	(No contraction)
He <u>is not</u> hungry.	He <u>isn't</u> hungry.
We <u>are not</u> hungry.	We <u>aren't</u> hungry.

➤ **B.** Rewrite each sentence with he negative form of the verb *to be*. Then rewrite the negative form as a contraction. The first one has been done for you.

1. She is tired of waiting.

   She is not tired of waiting. She isn't tired of waiting.

2. They are tourists from Spain.

   _____

3. The animal is active at night.

   _____

Student
Handbook

From Reading to Writing

Use with student text page 53.

Edit a Personal Narrative

➤ Use the checklist to edit the personal narrative you wrote in Chapter 4.

Editing Checklist for a Personal Narrative

Title of text: _____

What I did:

_____ **1.** I wrote a letter to a new pen pal. I remembered to

    a. _____ write the date.

    b. _____ use a greeting.

    c. _____ indent the body of my letter.

    d. _____ write a closing.

    e. _____ sign my letter.

_____ **2.** I described myself and my family. I remembered to

    a. _____ tell my age.

    b. _____ describe how I look.

    c. _____ tell about my daily activities.

    d. _____ tell where I live and what I like to do.

_____ **3.** I used the first-person pronouns *I, me, we,* and *us.*

_____ **4.** I used chronological transition words.

Across Content Areas

Use with student text page 53.

Understand and Use Symbols

A symbol is something that stands for something else. For example, the eagle is often a symbol of freedom.

Turkish kilim designs contain many symbols. One of these symbols is the **elibelinde.** It is a symbol of motherhood. Another symbol used on kilims is **ram's horn.** It is a symbol for power and heroism (acts of courage and great skill).

Think about things that could stand for motherhood and heroism in our culture.

Elibelinde

Ram's Horn

➤ Draw symbols for motherhood and heroism in the space below.

Name _____ Date _____

Build Vocabulary
Show Word Meaning

Use with student text page 55.

➤ Fill in the chart. Write a sentence that shows the meaning of each word. Then draw a picture that relates to each word.

Word	Meaning	Sentence	Picture
staring	looking at something continuously	She could not stop staring at the colorful paintings.	
puzzled	confused; not understanding		
whisper	speak softly and with a low voice		
lopsided	with one side larger than the other		
plump	full and round in shape		
parasol	a light umbrella that protects from the sun		
twinkling	shining		

Writing: Punctuation

Punctuate Dialogue

Use with student text page 64.

Dialogue is the exact words that characters say. Dialogue is shown by placing **quotation marks** ("...") around the words that are spoken.

Read the rules for punctuating dialogue in the chart.

Rules for Punctuating Dialogue	
Rule	**Examples**
Quotation marks always appear in pairs. They are placed before the first word said. They are also placed after the last word said.	"I just want the sickness to be over with," Sadako said unhappily.
Periods (.), commas (,), question marks (?), and exclamation points (!) are always placed inside quotation marks in dialogue.	Sadako was puzzled. "But how can that paper bird make me well?"
When a quotation is broken into two parts, two sets of quotation marks are used.	"Don't you remember that old story about the crane?" Chizuko asked. "It's supposed to live for a thousand years."

➤ **A.** Edit these sentences. Rewrite the sentences by adding the missing quotation marks. Some sentences may not need quotation marks. The first one has been done for you.

1. Thank you, Chizuko chan, she whispered. I'll never part with it.

"Thank you, Chizuko chan," she whispered. "I'll never part with it."

2. Now I have only nine hundred and ninety to make," Sadako said.

_____

3. A thousand! Her brother groaned. You're joking!

_____

4. After supper Mrs. Sasaki brought Mitsue and Eiji to the hospital.

_____

5. This is my choice, she said, because small ones are the most difficult to make.

_____

Elements of Literature

Use with student text page 65.

Understand Characterization and Motivation

Characterization is the way an author creates a character. Authors use dialogue, descriptions, actions, and thoughts to tell what a character is like. **Motivation** is the reason or reasons why a character acts the way he or she does.

Carlos studied hard. He wanted to get an A on the test. He wants to go to college and have a better life than his parents had.

Why does Carlos study so hard? His motivation is that he wants to go to college and have a better life than his parents.

➤ **A.** Think of a character. It can be a real person or someone that you make up. Fill in the chart to create your character.

Name of Character:
Description: (age, hair, clothes, height, and so on)
Characteristics: Examples: speaks fast; has a good attitude
Goal: (What does your character want to do?) Example: He wants to get an A on a test.
Actions: (What does your character do to try to reach his or her goal?) Example: He studies for five hours each night.
Motivation: (Why does he or she want to do it?) Example: He wants to go to college and have a better life than his parents.

➤ **B.** Write three sentences describing your character. Use the chart to help you.

_____

_____

_____

Name _____ Date _____

Word Study

Use with student text page 66.

Use Adjectives Ending in -ed

Adjectives are words that describe a person, place, or thing.

Anna has beautiful hair.

Beautiful is an adjective. It describes Anna's hair.

Some adjectives can be made by adding *-ed* to the simple form of a verb. The simple form of a verb is the verb without any endings. *Join* is a simple verb. You can make *join* an adjective by adding *-ed*.

They let go of their *joined* hands.

If a verb ends in *e*, just add *-d* to make the adjective.

➤ **A.** Write the *-ed* adjective forms for each of these verbs.

Verb	Adjective	Verb	Adjective
puzzle	*puzzled*	pack	
trouble		join	
surprise		need	
please			

➤ **B.** Complete the sentences with one of the adjectives in the chart.

1. He was _____ when the teacher asked the question.

2. I did very well on the test, so I am _____.

3. I added sugar to the tea, but it wasn't _____.

4. There were 100 people in the room. It was _____!

5. I was _____ when everyone yelled "Happy Birthday!"

6. Andreas's parents are _____ because his grades are not very good.

7. The six girls sang together. Their _____ voices were strong and joyful.

VISIONS A Activity Book • Copyright © Heinle

Grammar Focus

Use with student text page 66.

Recognize and Use Possessive Nouns

A **possessive noun** is a noun that shows who owns something. A singular noun is a noun that stands for one person or one thing. You form possessive nouns from singular nouns by adding an apostrophe and *-s* (**'s**) to it.

I used <u>Ramon's</u> bat.

In the sentence above, *Ramon's* is a singular possessive noun. Ramon *possesses,* or owns, the bat.

➤ Edit these sentences. Rewrite the sentences by correcting singular nouns that should be in the possessive form. Some of the sentences do not have errors.

1. That afternoon, Chizuko was Sadako first visitor.

   That afternoon, Chizuko was Sadako's first visitor. _____

2. With Chizuko help, she learned how to do the difficult parts.

   _____

3. He placed his pencils on the desk.

   _____

4. She has two brothers.

   _____

5. She borrowed her brothers coat.

   _____

6. He put the collar around the dog neck.

   _____

7. Please take off your little brother boots.

   _____

Name _____ Date _____

Grammar Focus

Use with student text page 66.

Recognize and Use Possessive Nouns: Regular and Irregular Noun Plurals

A **plural noun** is a noun that stands for more than one person or thing. Most singular nouns add an *-s* to form plural nouns *(cat—cats; girl—girls)*. You form most possessive nouns from plural nouns by adding an apostrophe (') after the word.

The <u>cats</u>' owner (plural noun: *cats*)   The <u>girls</u>' mother (plural noun: *girls*)

Some nouns form plurals in different ways. They are called **irregular nouns.** *Woman* is an irregular noun. Its plural form is *women*.

You form the possessive form of irregular plural nouns by adding an apostrophe and an *-s* (**'s**) to the end of the word: (women**'s**).

Singular Regular Nouns	Plural Regular Nouns	Singular Irregular Nouns	Plural Irregular Nouns
crane	cranes	man	men
teacher	teachers	child	children
doctor	doctors	man	men

➤ Edit these sentences. Rewrite the sentences by writing the plural nouns in the possessive form. Some of the sentences do not have errors.

1. The cranes necks are very long.

    The cranes' necks are very long.
    _____

2. The children's ball is lost.

    _____

3. All of my teachers were happy with my progress.

    _____

4. The mens' team won all of its games.

    _____

5. The three doctors' talked with us.

    _____

6. Have you seen the three doctors bags?

    _____

Student
Handbook

VISIONS A Activity Book • Copyright © Heinle

From Reading to Writing

Use with student text page 67.

Edit a Fictional Narrative

➤ Use the checklist to edit the fictional narrative you wrote in Chapter 5.

Editing Checklist for a Fictional Narrative

Title of narrative: _____

What I did:

_____ 1. I described the setting—the time and place of my story.

_____ 2. I used characterization to tell readers about my characters.

_____ 3. I put the events in my story in chronological order.

_____ 4. I included dialogue with quotation marks.

_____ 5. I connected the events by using words to show what happens next, such as *soon, next,* and *finally.*

_____ 6. I used proper punctuation throughout my story.

_____ **a.** I put commas, periods, question marks, and exclamation points within quotes.

_____ **b.** I used apostrophes correctly.

_____ 7. I indented my paragraphs.

Across Content Areas

Use with student text page 67.

Summarize an Article

➤ Read the article about origami.

The Art of Origami

Origami is the art of folding paper. The word *origami* comes from the Japanese words *oru* (to fold) and *kami* (paper). It is believed that paper was invented in China around the year A.D. 105. Shortly after the Chinese made paper, they began folding it into different shapes.

Paper-making came to Japan in the 500s, and the art of origami quickly became a part of Japanese culture. The Japanese soon learned how to make very detailed and beautiful forms.

Japanese nobles (people of high positions) used origami as part of some traditions and ceremonies (events held for special purposes). Some of the origami forms used in the ceremonies had symbolic meanings that stood for important things in the Japanese culture. Some nobles even presented gifts in different origami forms.

Today, people all over the world enjoy the art of origami. Thousands of amazing origami forms can be made from paper. Some almost look like stone or wooden sculptures!

➤ **A.** Summarize the article.

Origami is the art of folding paper. It came to Japan

_____

_____

➤ **B.** How is this article similar to and different from "Sadako and the Thousand Paper Cranes"?

_____

_____

Build Vocabulary

Use with student text page 77.

Use Context Clues to Understand Words

Context clues are words and sentences around a specific word. Context clues can help you learn new words. Look at this word from "Here Is the Southwestern Desert":

When the cat <u>spied</u> the mouse, he ran after it.

The second part of the sentence lets you guess that <u>spied</u> means "saw."

➤ **A.** Read the context clues in each sentence. Choose the letter of the definition that fits each underlined word.

> **Definitions**
> **a.** a place that provides protection
> **b.** attack by jumping quickly on something
> **c.** dry
> **d.** sat in one spot
> **e.** sharp, pointy needles
> **f.** goes after something
> **g.** enjoy the sun while sitting or lying down
> **h.** uncovered

1. ___*h*___ Gina and Sam <u>unearthed</u> some rocks when they were digging in the yard.

2. _____ A nest is a good <u>shelter</u> for baby birds.

3. _____ If you touch the <u>spines</u> on a cactus, you can hurt yourself.

4. _____ The bird <u>perched</u> on a fence post and began to sing.

5. _____ The bobcat runs fast as it <u>chases</u> the animal.

6. _____ Cats will <u>pounce</u> on a moving string.

7. _____ Turtles <u>bask</u>, because it makes their bodies warmer.

8. _____ A desert is a <u>rainless</u> place, so only plants that do not need water grow there.

➤ **B.** Underline the word that does not fit in each list.

1. unearthed, discovered, buried, found

2. shelter, outdoors, home, protection

3. soft, prickly, needles, sharp

4. sat, rested, walk, perched

5. hunts, pursues, chases, ignores

6. pounce, attack, encourage, jump

7. bask, warm, work, sunlight

8. dry, desert, wet, rainless

Writing: Capitalization

Use with student text page 88.

Capitalize Words and Punctuate Series of Adjectives

Capitalize First Words

The first word in a sentence always has a capital (larger) letter. This is usually true for the first word of sentences in poems.

Here is the cactus
that is covered with spines
and can live without rain
for a very long time.

The other lines in this poem do *not* start with a capital letter. *Here* is the beginning of the sentence. The sentence does not end until you see a period.

A. ➤ Read this section of "Here Is the Southwestern Desert." Circle the two letters that should be capitalized.

here is the hawk
that perches on the cactus
that is covered with spines
and can live without rain
for a very long time.
here is the southwestern desert.

Punctuate Sentences with Adjectives

Adjectives describe people, places, or things. Two or more adjectives in a sentence are separated by commas.

I love the cool, clear nights of the desert.

The small, fast, and sneaky bobcat is a good hunter.

A comma is not placed after the last adjective that comes before the word it describes. In the sentences above, a comma is not placed after *clear* and *sneaky*.

B. ➤ Edit these sentences. Add commas to separate the adjectives. The first one has been done for you.

1. The cactus has long**,** sharp**,** pointy spines.

2. The hawk flies in high beautiful circles.

3. The high dry and cold desert has few plants.

4. Lizards slide on the sand on their short thick rough legs.

5. Many animals dig cool safe shelters under the sand.

6. The coyotes' high sad cries are heard across the cold empty desert.

Elements of Literature

Use with student text page 89.

Recognize Free Verse

A poem that is written in **free verse** does not use rhymes. Rhymes are words with the same ending sound, like *run* and *sun*.

A. ➤ Read the lines. If it they end in rhymes, write *R* in the space. If they do not end in rhymes, write *F* in the space.

1. There once was a wizard

who had a pet lizard.

_____*R*_____

2. The coyotes cried

like lost children.

_____

3. The badger digs in the earth

with powerful energy.

_____

4. As it runs along the ground,

the roadrunner makes its "beep-beep" sound.

_____

5. Here comes the cool desert moon.

The animals will be coming out soon.

_____

6. When the hot sun bakes the sand,

the animals dream about the moon.

_____

7. The holes in the desert are empty.

The owl will dig no more.

_____

8. The snake puts its tongue in the air

to see if there's some food out there.

_____

Word Study

Use with student text page 90.

Recognize Word Origins

The desert of the southwestern part of the United States is next to Mexico. In Mexico, people speak Spanish. Many of the words we use in English to describe the desert come from Spanish.

Word	Meaning
arroyo	a stream
canyon	a narrow valley with steep sides
armadillo	a small animal covered with hard shells
mesa	a high, flat piece of land
mustangs	wild horses
puma	(from Quechua) a large, brown desert cat
ranch	a very large farm in the western U.S.
iguana	a type of lizard

➤ Complete the sentences. Use the words in the chart.

1. The badger drank from the ___arroyo_____ that ran through the desert.

2. A herd of _____, without riders, ran across the wide-open desert.

3. Like other lizards, the _____ likes to bask in the sun.

4. We climbed to the top of the _____ to get a better view.

5. Few animals can eat the _____ because its shell is so hard.

6. On each side of the _____, the cliffs were high above us.

7. The _____ is a cat that is hard to see, because it is brown like the desert.

8. We stayed on a _____ during our desert vacation.

Grammar Focus

Use with student text page 90.

Identify the Simple Present Tense

A **present tense verb** describes an action that is generally true or that happens regularly.

He <u>likes</u> chocolate ice cream.

I <u>eat</u> breakfast every morning.

When the subject of a simple present tense verb is *he, she,* or *it,* add an *-s* to the end of most verbs.

Three verbs are irregular when the subject is *he, she,* or *it.*

Simple Present Tense			
Subject	**Simple Verb**	**Subject**	**Simple Verb + -s**
I, You, We, They	eat	He, She, It	eats
Subject	**Simple Verb**	**Subject**	**Irregular -s Form**
I, You, We, They	do go have	He, She, It	does goes has

A. ➤ Underline the subject in each sentence. Put two underlines below the simple present tense verb.

1. <u>She</u> <u>wants</u> to be a doctor someday.

2. I have no more homework.

3. He feels cold.

4. They travel to Europe each summer.

5. It snows here in February.

B. ➤ Underline the correct simple present tense verb in each sentence.

1. They (ride/rides) to the movies every Friday night.

2. It (seem/seems) like we have been waiting forever.

3. I (play/plays) soccer after school.

4. He (do/does) homework every night.

Grammar Focus

Use with student text page 90.

Find the Subject of Simple Present Tense Verbs

A. ➤ Underline the subject in each sentence.

1. <u>Pablo and Michela</u> go to the Thanksgiving Day football game.
2. It rains a lot in the spring.
3. Sofia runs for the track team.
4. Jorge smiles when he tells jokes.
5. You cook better than my other friends.

B. ➤ Complete each sentence with a subject that will go with the simple present tense of the verb. The first one has been done for you.

1. ___*I*___ like to run every morning.
2. _____ is nice to wake up and go outside.
3. In my family, _____ exercise every day.
4. I see my father as _____ walks in the door.
5. When my parents can cook together, _____ enjoy it.

C. ➤ Write three sentences in the simple present tense. Tell about people you know and what they do regularly.

1. _____

    _____

2. _____

    _____

3. _____

    _____

Student
Handbook

Name _____   Date _____

From Reading to Writing

Use with student text page 91.

Write a Poem About the Environment

Imagine that you are going to write a poem about a place. Describe what it looks like, what it feels like, what it sounds like, and who or what lives there.

A. ➤ Fill in the chart to organize the details in your poem.

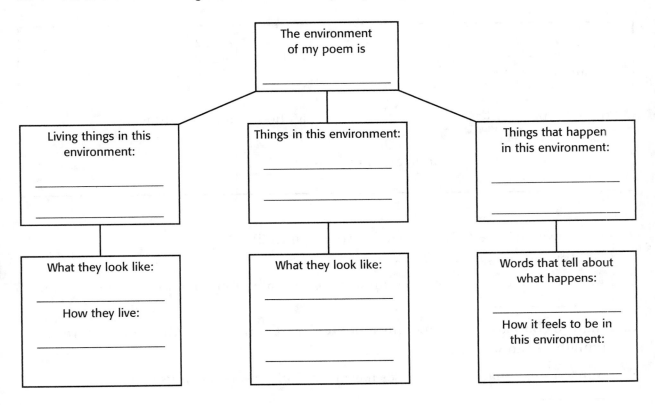

The environment of my poem is _____

Living things in this environment:
_____
_____

Things in this environment:
_____
_____

Things that happen in this environment:
_____
_____

What they look like:
_____
How they live:
_____

What they look like:
_____
_____
_____

Words that tell about what happens:
_____
How it feels to be in this environment:
_____

B. ➤ Write four lines that could be part of your poem. You may use words that rhyme or words that do not rhyme.

_____

_____

_____

_____

Across Content Areas

Use with student text page 91.

Use Audiovisual Resources

Imagine that you are giving a presentation on the desert. You can use many audiovisual resources to make your presentation more interesting. Look at the audiovisual resources listed. Use the list to complete the statements. Sometimes there is more than one correct answer.

an audio CD or
an audiocassette

a video

the Internet

a photograph or a drawing

a diagram or a chart

1. I want my audience to hear what a coyote sounds like.
   I can use _____ .

2. I want my audience to see some interesting web sites about life in the desert. I can use _____ .

3. I want to compare the temperature of the desert at noon with the temperature at midnight. I can use _____ .

4. I want to show that some cactuses have beautiful flowers. I can use
   _____ .

5. I want to show a scientist talking about the desert environment. I can use
   _____ .

Build Vocabulary

Use with student text page 93.

Take Notes as You Read

While you are reading, you may see a word you do not know. You can learn the word better if you write down your ideas about its meaning. You can use context clues and your experience to do this.

A. ➤ Read the passage. On the note card, write what you think each underlined word means.

In my <u>neighborhood</u>, there is a noisy train. It is an <u>elevated</u> train that runs above the ground. People would like to have an <u>underground</u> train. A train that runs under the street would be quieter.

People's lives would <u>improve</u> with more peace and quiet. Life would be a lot better. The city should <u>design</u> a new train that runs underground. My <u>opinion</u> is that it would not be too hard. Now, most people <u>pretend</u> they do not mind the noise. But it is hard to make believe that such a loud noise is not really there.

Word	Meaning
neighborhood	1. the place where someone lives
elevated	2.
underground	3.
improve	4.
design	5.
opinion	6.
pretend	7.

B. ➤ Match the words with their meanings. Compare your answers with the chart above.

_____ 1. **neighborhood**   **a.** above the ground, high up

_____ 2. **elevated**   **b.** a plan

_____ 3. **underground**   **c.** the area where someone lives

_____ 4. **improve**   **d.** what someone believes

_____ 5. **design**   **e.** below the earth's surface

_____ 6. **opinion**   **f.** act as though something is true, but it isn't true

_____ 7. **pretend**   **g.** make better

VISIONS A Activity Book • Copyright © Heinle

Name _____ Date _____

Writing: Capitalization

Use with student text page 102.

Capitalize Place Names and Use Italics

Place names include the names of countries, states, cities, towns, roads, and streets. They begin with a capital letter.

Fifth **A**venue, **N**ew **Y**ork **C**ity

A. ➤ Find the place name that should be capitalized in each sentence. Write it correctly.

1. Rita's family came from mexico. _*Mexico*_____

2. The train station is on main Street. _____

3. My aunt lives in vermont. _____

4. It is a long drive from chicago to New York. _____

5. The White House is in washington, D.C. _____

B. ➤ Edit these sentences. Rewrite the sentences by capitalizing the place names.

1. You can drive on the highway from florida to new Jersey.
   _You can drive on the highway from Florida to New Jersey._____

2. The cities of atlanta and Los Angeles have a lot of cars.

   _____

3. Please visit me at my new home in springfield, massachusetts.

   _____

Use Italics

Writers sometimes use italics (slanted writing that looks *like this*) to get readers to pay special attention.

After all, it is really *their* subway station.

By putting the word *their* in italics, the writer is saying he cares about people who live near the subway station.

C. ➤ Underline the word before each sentence that should be put in italics.

1. (<u>first,</u> to)   I want to enjoy my first subway trip.

2. (never, on)   I have never been on a subway before.

3. (my, very)   My friend said subways can be very noisy.

VISIONS Unit 2 • Chapter 2 Subway Architect

VISIONS A Activity Book • Copyright © Heinle

Elements of Literature

Use with student text page 103.

Understand Character Motivation

Motivation is the reason why a character does something. There are many motivations for what characters do. For example, a character may go to bed because he is sleepy.

➤ Each box shows what a character is doing. In the empty box next to it, write the motivation for what he or she is doing. You may make up a reason.

Action	**Motivation**
1. He wanted to leave because	
2. She enjoyed building homes for people because	
3. Linda and her friends liked taking the subway to school because	
4. Joey felt he had to call his friend because	
5. Mike worked hard on his bike because	

Word Study

Use with student text page 104.

Learn About the Prefix *sub-*

A **prefix** is a group of letters that added to the beginning of a word. A prefix can change the meaning of the word.

The prefix *sub-* means "under" or "below." When *sub-* is added to the word *way*, the word *subway* is formed. *Way* means "a path or road." The word *subway* means "trains that travel on a path below the ground."

A. ➤ Add the prefix *sub-* to the beginning of each word. Write the new word on the line in each space.

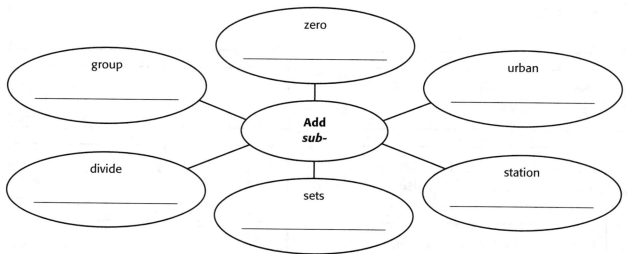

B. ➤ Complete the sentences by adding *sub-* to each underlined word. Use the chart.

1. The farmer will <u>divide</u> his farm into pieces of land.

   Next, he will ___*subdivide*___ them into smaller pieces of land.

2. Yesterday, the temperature was near <u>zero</u>.

   It will be even colder today, with _____ temperatures.

3. There is a big police <u>station</u> in the center of town.

   A few blocks away, there is a smaller _____.

4. A large <u>group</u> went into the auditorium.

   Then a _____ went into one of the smaller rooms to play music.

5. The pens and pencils are a <u>set</u> of writing tools.

   The pencils are a smaller _____ of the group of writing tools.

6. An <u>urban</u> area is in the city.

   A _____ area is outside the city.

Grammar Focus

Identify Questions

Questions are sentences that ask for an answer. Questions often begin with words like *who, what, where, when, how,* or *why.* A question ends with a question mark (**?**).

What are you doing Saturday afternoon**?**

A. ➤ Read each sentence. In the space after each sentence, write *Q* if it is a question. Write *N* if the sentence is *not* a question. The first one has been done for you.

1. Where did I put my keys? _*Q*_____

2. Did you see Mike at school today? _____

3. I don't know how I am going to finish this work. _____

4. Where is my backpack? _____

5. Why does it always rain on the weekend? _____

6. We will go out when it stops raining. _____

7. When do you want to go to the movies? _____

8. I just went to the movies. _____

B. ➤ Complete each sentence with the correct punctuation. The first one has been done for you.

1. What is that girl's name_*?*___

2. I don't know what her name is____

3. Please tell me what time it is____

4. What time is it____

5. I will decide what to wear today____

6. What should I wear____

7. You are a good athlete____

8. How did you become such a good athlete____

Grammar Focus

Use with student text page 104.

Write Questions with the Present Tense of *Be*

Suppose a sentence is in the simple present tense and the verb is *be*. You can turn this sentence into a question by changing the order of the subject and the form of *be*.

In the examples below the subject is underlined two times. The *be* form of the verb is underlined one time.

Sentence: <u>The student</u> <u>is</u> in the sixth grade.

Question: <u>Is</u> <u>the student</u> in the sixth grade?

Sentence: <u>Texans</u> <u>are</u> very friendly.

Question: <u>Are</u> <u>Texans</u> very friendly?

➤ Rewrite the sentences as questions by reversing the order of the subject and the verb. The first one has been done for you.

1. Our report is due.

   Is our report due? _____

2. Fairuza is in the class.

   _____

3. The class is over.

   _____

4. Jane is next door.

   _____

5. Maya is in your class.

   _____

6. I am a good writer.

   _____

7. We are sure about the directions.

   _____

8. They are from out of town.

   _____

Student
Handbook

From Reading to Writing

Use with student text page 105.

Outline a Personal Narrative

A **personal narrative** is a story you write about yourself.

A. ➤ Fill in the outline to help you organize your thoughts for a personal narrative. Each major section (I, II, and III) of the outline gives information for a paragraph. Write about a hobby, such as playing a sport or acting in plays.

> **My Hobby**
>
> **I. Main Idea: What my hobby is and why I like it**
>
> **A.** My hobby is _____
>
> **B.** Why I like this hobby _____
>
> **II. Main Idea: Description of my hobby**
>
> **A.** What my hobby is like:
>
>   **1.** Things I need for my hobby _____
>
>   **2.** Where I can do my hobby _____
>
> **B.** People I can share my hobby with _____
>
> **III. Main Idea: How my hobby makes me feel**
>
> **A.** Why I think my hobby is interesting:
>
>   **1.** Why my hobby is difficult or easy _____
>
>   **2.** Why my hobby is fun _____
>
> **B.** Why others might enjoy my hobby _____

B. ➤ Write at least three sentences for the first paragraph of your personal narrative. Use the outline to help you.

' _____

_____

_____

_____

Across Content Areas

Use with student text page 105.

Design a Mural

Most subway stations have long walls. These walls are great for painting **murals** (paintings on walls).

A. ➤ Write ideas for a mural in your town in each box.

Things About My Town I Like
1. _____
2. _____
3. _____

How I Can Show These Things in a Mural
1. _____
2. _____
3. _____

B. ➤ Draw a mural that shows what your town is like. Use your ideas from the boxes to help you.

Build Vocabulary

Use with student text page 107.

Use Definitions and Recognize Nouns

Use Definitions

➤ Study the following definitions.

Word and Definition
respect show concern about the importance of something
filth dirt and garbage
choke stop breathing because of a block in the air passage
shivered shook in the body from cold
appeal ask for help
crows makes a loud cry
plight a difficult situation
eager excited to do something
shine add light
leads shows the way

➤ Complete the sentences. Use the words in the box. The first one has been done for you.

1. We __*shivered*__ when we played outside in the snow.

2. The children are always _____ to play.

3. The rooster _____ loudly every morning.

4. It is sad to think about the _____ of homeless people.

5. The person holding the flag _____ the parade.

6. People should _____ one another by listening when someone is talking.

7. Don't litter. There is too much _____ in the street.

8. My cat got some food stuck in his throat and started to _____.

9. The people will _____ for help from the government.

10. Please _____ the flashlight over here.

Writing: Punctuation

Use with student text page 114.

Use Quotation Marks with Questions and Exclamations

Quotation marks ("...") are placed before and after the exact words that a character says. Here are some examples of questions inside quotation marks:

"How could I get across the Eastern Sea?"

"Won't you take pity on us?" the rooster pleaded.

A. ➤ Where does the question mark go for questions that use quotation marks?

_____

_____

Here are some examples of exclamations (sentences that express strong emotion and end in **!**) that use quotation marks:

"Help us, sister sun!"

"Cock-a-doodle do!" crowed the rooster.

B. ➤ Where does the exclamation point go for exclamations that use quotation marks?

_____

_____

C. ➤ Edit these sentences. Rewrite the sentences by placing quotation marks in the correct places.

1. How could I get across the Eastern Sea? asked the rooster.

_____

_____

2. How can you ask me to come back? said the sun.

_____

_____

3. You know I had to leave! said the sun.

_____

_____

4. I can help, too! said the bluebird.

_____

_____

Elements of Literature

Review Personification

Personification describes a thing or an animal as if it were a person. For example, a writer uses personification when he or she writes about an animal that talks or has feelings and thoughts.

➤ Read the following story.

The Cat and the Fish

A sailor, who was on a long trip, took a singing cat with him to keep him company. All of a sudden, a bad storm started. The sailor's ship broke into pieces. The sailor started to swim to the shore. The cat did not know how to swim.

A fish saw the cat trying to swim. The fish put the cat on his back and took him safely to the shore.

They came to the shore. The cat could not see, because he had so much water in his eyes. So he did not know who had saved him. The cat thanked the fish many times, asking how he could thank him more.

The fish said, "I need more food. I am having trouble finding food in these rough waters."

The cat said, "That is no problem at all. As soon as my eyes are better, I will catch some fish for you to eat."

The fish became very angry at the cat. He grabbed him and carried the cat back into the water, where he left him.

➤ Answer these questions about the fable.

1. How is the cat like a person?

_____

2. How is the fish like a person?

_____

3. Give an example of something the fish might say to the cat when he became angry.

_____

_____

4. Give an example of something the cat might say when the fish threw him into the water.

_____

_____

Word Study

Use with student text page 116.

Study Multiple Meaning Words

Sometimes words have more than one meaning. For example:

I play on a soccer team.

I acted in the school play.

In the first sentence, *play* means "take part in a game or an event." In the second sentence, *play* means "a drama performance."

A. ➤ Circle the letter that shows the meaning of the underlined word in each sentence. Use context clues to help you. The first one has been done for you.

1. She grew more unhappy.
   a. got bigger
   (b.) became

2. He set her down in a safe place.
   a. in a low place
   b. sad

3. If I had left you there, they would have hurt you.
   a. kept
   b. opposite of right

4. If we could appeal to her, perhaps she would help us.
   a. nice-looking
   b. call for help

5. I will lead you there.
   a. show the way
   b. a wire for electricity

6. The rooster was riding on the duck.
   a. to go under
   b. a type of bird

7. We cannot see to find food.
   a. understand
   b. use our eyes

8. Call me when you need light.
   a. the opposite of heavy
   b. the opposite of darkness

9. Get ready to cross the sea.
   a. go across
   b. angry

10. The rooster crows when the sun rises.
    a. black birds
    b. makes a sound

Grammar Focus

Use with student text page 116.

Use Object Pronouns

Some sentences have objects. The objects receive the action of a verb. Objects can be nouns or pronouns (words that take the place of nouns).

The rooster asked the <u>sun</u> for help.

The action is *asked*. The *sun* receives the action of the verb. The word *sun* is the object.

Here is another example:

He called Diana. Then he asked <u>her</u> for help.

The pronoun *her* takes the place of *Diana*. *Her* is the object of the second sentence. It is an object pronoun.

Object Pronouns	Example
me	She hugged me.
you (one person)	I will call you today.
him	They need him at work.
her	I like her very much.
it	I heard it.
us	They visit us often.
you (more than one person)	Books help you learn.
them	Let's go see them now.

➤ Underline the correct object pronoun or pronouns in each sentence. Use the chart to help you. The first one has been done for you.

1. She lived close to (he/<u>him</u>).

2. They do not know (we/us).

3. They did not thank (she/her).

4. The Emperor did not feel bad for (we/us).

5. He left (I/me) there.

6. They would have hurt (you and I/you and me).

7. The animals did not know (they/them).

8. They talked about it with (he and she/him and her).

Grammar Focus

Use with student text page 116.

Use Pronoun Referents

A **pronoun referent** is the noun that the pronoun replaces.

He ate ice cream. He ate it.

The word *it* refers back to *ice cream*. The word *it* is the object pronoun, and *ice cream* is the pronoun referent.

➤ Read both sentences. Then underline the pronoun referent in the first sentence. Underline the pronoun in the second sentence twice.

1. Long ago the <u>earth</u> was beautiful.

   People didn't take care of <u>it</u>.

2. The people burned wood and trash.

   Jade Emperor was angry with them.

3. He took his daughter away.

   He said, "You are safe now."

4. People couldn't see anything.

   The sun wasn't there to help them.

5. The animals said, "We need light."

   They wanted the sun to help.

6. The animals asked the sun for help.

   But the sun didn't want to give it because the earth was too polluted.

7. The animals said, "Oh, please help!"

   The sun said, "Well, OK. I will help you."

8. The rooster promised to call the sun every morning.

   "Trust me," said the rooster.

9. The sun and the rooster made a bargain.

   They have kept it, and that's why the rooster crows at sunrise.

Student
Handbook

From Reading to Writing

Use with student text page 117.

Write a Fable

Fables are stories that teach a lesson. Most fables use personification. Remember that personification means that a thing or an animal acts as if it was a person.

To write a fable, choose an animal that can be your main character. Then think of the lesson you would like to teach. For example, you might want to teach that it is good to be helpful to others.

A. ➤ Write a list of things that show what people can do that makes them different from animals.

Qualities People Have

_____

_____

_____

_____

_____

_____

_____

_____

B. ➤ Write sentences that show how the animal you chose for your fable is like a person. Then, write the lesson that you would like to teach in your fable.

_____

_____

_____

_____

_____

VISIONS **Unit 2 • Chapter 3** Why the Rooster Crows at Sunrise

Across Content Areas

Use with student text page 117.

Compare and Contrast Fables

Compare and contrast "Why the Rooster Crows at Sunrise" with the fable on page 59 of this book, "The Cat and the Fish." Or you may compare and contrast "Why the Rooster Crows at Sunrise" with another fable that you know.

A. ➤ Fill in the Venn Diagram. Write how "Why the Rooster Crows at Sunrise" is different in the left circle part. Write how "The Cat and the Fish" or another fable is different in the right circle part. Write how both fables are similar in the overlapping circle parts.

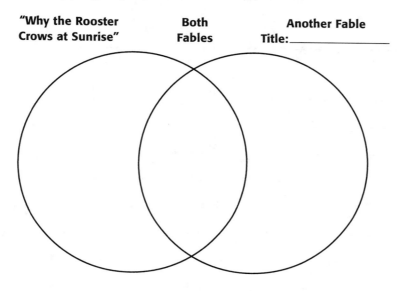

"Why the Rooster Crows at Sunrise"   **Both Fables**   **Another Fable Title:_____**

B. ➤ Answer the questions. Use the Venn Diagram.

1. How are the characters similar and different?

_____

2. How are the characters' relationships similar and different?

_____

3. How are the problems in the fables similar and different?

_____

4. How are the endings similar and different?

_____

5. How is the organization of the fables similar and different?

_____

Build Vocabulary

Use with student text page 119.

Put Words into Groups and Understand Verbs

Put Words into Groups

When you put words into groups, you connect them to other words. For example, the word *Juan* is Spanish for the name *John*. It could belong to any of these groups:

Spanish words   First names

Men's names   Boys' names

➤ Study the definitions.

Word and Definition
Mexican a person from Mexico   **troughs** long and narrow ditches
tío the Spanish word for "uncle"   **spotted** saw
wandered walked around   **bodega** the Spanish word for "shop"
trowel a small tool used to dig up soil   **Salvadoran** a person from El Salvador
seed something that is planted   **stare** look for a long time
pueblo the Spanish word for "village"

A. ➤ Fill in the chart. Use the words in the box.

Names of Groups of People	Spanish Words	Verbs (Action Words)	Words That Have to Do With Gardens

Parts of Speech: Verbs

Verbs are words that show action.

I <u>called</u> his name.

B. ➤ Complete the sentences. Use the verbs in the box.

1. He _____ from chair to chair, looking for a place to sit down.

2. He _____ a butterfly from very far away.

3. It is not polite to _____ at people.

Writing: Spelling

Use with student text page 128.

Use Homophones

Homophones are words that are pronounced the same, but have different spellings and meanings. Look at the homophones that are underlined in the sentences below.

He didn't want strangers to <u>hear</u> his mistakes.

He'd been a farmer, but <u>here</u> he couldn't work.

➤ Study the definitions for each group of homophones.

---

1. **one** the first number
   won did the best

2. **buy** get something that is for sale
   by near
   bye short for "good-bye"

3. **stair** a step up or down
   stare look for a long time

4. **hear** listen with ears
   here in this place

5. **two** the number after "one"
   too also
   to in the direction of

6. **their** belongs to the
   there not here
   they're they are

➤ Complete the sentences. Use the definitions in the box to help you. The first one has been done for you.

1. I ate _____one_____ hot dog at the baseball game. (one/won)

2. Where did you _____ your jeans? (buy/by/bye)

3. People often _____ at movie stars. (stair/stare)

4. There are not any places to rest _____. (hear/here)

5. We moved _____ years ago. (two/too/to)

6. She asked me to take him _____. (their/there/they're)

Elements of Literature

Use with student text page 129.

Review Theme

The **theme** of a story is the main idea. The story of "Gonzalo" begins with this sentence:

> The older you are, the younger you get when you move to the United States.

What makes people feel younger when they are really getting older? What happens to people when they move to a new place? The writer wants us to think about these ideas.

➤ Answer the questions about the theme that is in the above sentence. Give your opinions. There are no right or wrong answers.

1. Is it easier for children or adults to move to a new place? Why?

   _____

   _____

   _____

2. What is the hardest thing about moving to a new place?

   _____

   _____

3. In the story "Gonzalo," Tío Juan cannot understand what people say on TV. In what other ways do people have trouble with language in a new country?

   _____

   _____

   _____

4. Gonzalo learned English on the playground and by watching TV. Do you think this is a good way to learn English? Why or why not?

   _____

   _____

   _____

5. What does this sentence mean? "The older you are, the younger you get when you move to the United States."

   _____

   _____

   _____

Word Study

Use with student text page 130.

Study Multiple Meaning Words

Sometimes words are spelled the same, but they have more than one meaning. Look at this example from "Gonzalo":

He didn't want a <u>stranger</u> to hear his mistakes.

Here, the word *stranger* means "a person you do not know." Now look at this sentence:

The movie about the elephant that could fly was <u>stranger</u> to me than other movies I have seen.

Here, the word *stranger* means "something that is different." When you read a new word, carefully read the sentence to understand its meaning.

➤ Study the following words. Then, read each sentence and write the correct definition in the space. The first one has been done for you.

1. block
   a. a cube, sometimes used as a toy
   b. an area surrounded by four streets
   c. to stop something
   He lives three <u>blocks</u> away. __*b*__

2. kid
   a. a baby goat
   b. a child
   He is an adult, but he behaves like a <u>kid</u>. _____

3. shade
   a. not sunny
   b. something on a window that shuts out the sun
   c. color
   The leaves were different <u>shades</u> of green. _____

4. row
   a. a straight line
   b. move a boat
   My uncle planted the seeds in a <u>row</u>. _____

5. flew
   a. moved through the air
   b. moved quickly
   When Gonzalo noticed his uncle was missing, he <u>flew</u> down the street. _____

Grammar Focus

Use with student text page 130.

Recognize Regular Comparative Adjectives

Adjectives are words that describe nouns (names of people, places, or things). Sometimes we use adjectives to compare one thing to another.

Gonzalo is a <u>smart</u> boy.

The word *smart* is an adjective.

Gonzalo is <u>smarter</u> than José.

The word *smarter* is a comparative adjective. It compares Gonzalo to José.

For most short words, add *-er* to the adjective to make a comparative adjective. For most longer words, add the word *more*.

Adjective	Comparative Adjective	Adjective	Comparative Adjective
young	younger	dark	darker
focused	more focused	small	smaller
confused	more confused	familiar	more familiar
hard	harder	old	older

A. ➤ Write the underlined adjectives as comparative adjectives.

1. Gonzalo was <u>young</u>. He was _____ than his sister.

2. Juan was <u>focused</u> on doing a good job. He was _____ than I was.

3. My uncle was <u>confused</u>. He was _____ than before.

4. Life in the United States was <u>hard</u>. It was _____ than life in our country.

B. ➤ Edit this paragraph. On the lines, write the comparative adjectives by adding *-er* or *more* to each underlined adjective.

Guatemala is a small country. It is <u>small</u> than Mexico. Gonzalo is from Guatemala.
₁
His mother and father are <u>old</u> than Juan. His brothers are <u>young</u> than Gonzalo.
₂ ₃
Gonzalo is getting <u>smart</u> every day.
₄

1. _____   2. _____

3. _____   4. _____

Name _____ Date _____

Grammar Focus

Use with student text page 130.

Use Regular Comparative Adjectives

Writers use comparative adjectives to show how things compare to each other. Comparative adjectives help to make writing more *precise* (carefully written).

The dog is <u>big</u>.

The dog is <u>bigger than a small horse</u>.

The second sentence is more **precise.** It gives a better idea of how big the dog is.

➤ Complete the sentences with a word or phrase from the box.

I thought it would be
a picture
a house
art
the point of a pencil
a street full of people

1. The garden is <u>more beautiful</u> than _____.

2. The house was <u>more crowded</u> than _____.

3. The homework was <u>easier</u> than _____.

4. The plant was <u>taller</u> than _____.

5. The seeds were <u>smaller</u> than _____.

6. Math is <u>harder</u> than _____.

Student
Handbook

From Reading to Writing

Use with student text page 131.

A. ➤ Use the checklist to edit the story you wrote in Chapter 4.

Editing Checklist for Narrative Fiction

_____ **1.** I chose a person who learned to do something.

_____ **2.** I explained what they learned.

_____ **3.** My story has a beginning, a middle, and an end.

_____ **4.** I wrote details that shows how the person learned.

_____ **5.** I used comparative adjectives to show how the person changed.

_____ **6.** I read the story aloud to see how it sounded.

_____ **7.** I gave my story a title.

B. ➤ Write what you could have done differently or better in your story. Give at least two examples.

_____

_____

_____

_____

_____

_____

_____

_____

Across Content Areas

Use with student text page 131.

Complete an Outline

Plants have three main parts: leaves, stems, and roots. Each part is important for the plant's growth. Leaves can be many colors, but they are usually green. Leaves come in many shapes and sizes. The leaves of the plant make food that is carried to all of the parts of the plant.

The stem of the plant is the way the plant carries nutrients (things that help the plant grow) and water from the roots to the leaves. The stem holds up the leaves and flowers.

The roots of the plant go under the ground. The plant takes water from the ground through the roots. The roots also give the plant nutrients from the ground.

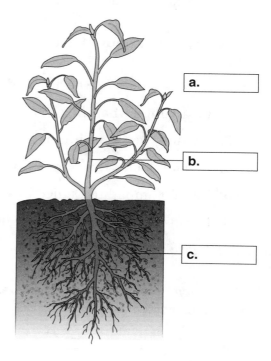

a.

b.

c.

➤ Fill in the outline with information you learned from reading the article.

I. Parts of Plants

   A. leaves

      1. usually green

      2. _____

      3. _____

   B. _____

      1. _____

      2. _____

   C. _____

      1. _____

      2. _____

      3. _____

Build Vocabulary

Use with student text page 133.

Find Synonyms and Use Pronouns

Find Synonyms

Synonyms are words that have similar meanings. A synonym can be a meaning for another word.

Carlos felt <u>puzzled</u> as he looked at the math lesson. He told his teacher he was <u>confused</u>.

The words *puzzled* and *confused* are synonyms.

A. ➤ Match the underlined word in each sentence to its synonym. Read the sentences carefully. They will help you understand the words.

Word in a Sentence

1. __*d*__ Snakes <u>slither</u> on the ground.

2. _____ There are many living <u>creatures</u> that make their homes in the forest.

3. _____ Animals will <u>crawl</u> up rocks to get at food.

4. _____ There were <u>swarms</u> of ants at the picnic.

5. _____ The stars sparkle as they <u>twinkle</u> at night.

6. _____ Eagles are <u>predators</u> that hunt and eat mice.

Synonym

a. climb

b. large groups

c. shine

d. slide

e. killers

f. animals

Parts of Speech: Use Pronouns

Pronouns are words that take the place of nouns. Nouns are names for people, places, and things.

In the sentence "Kiara went to the movies," *Kiara* can be replaced by the pronoun *she*. Other pronouns are *I, you, he, it, we,* and *they*.

B. ➤ Underline the pronoun in each sentence.

1. The television was on, so I watched <u>it.</u>

2. Anaka and Grace moved to a city that they liked.

3. Is Elizabeth your name, or do you have a nickname?

4. Matt took a shower before he left.

5. Wassim and I bought popcorn before we went to the movies.

6. My name is Corianne, but I like to be called Cori.

Writing: Punctuation

Use with student text page 140.

Use Commas with Nouns in a Series

Commas are used when there is a list of *more than two* things. In the sentence below, there is a comma after the words *snakes* and *crocodiles*.

Snakes**,** crocodiles**,** and lizards sleep near the river.

➤ Edit these sentences. Rewrite the sentences by adding commas where they are needed. If the sentence is correct, write *correct*.

1. They creep crawl and fly.

   They creep, crawl, and fly.

2. The rain forests are alive with animals bugs and birds.

   _____

   _____

3. Some animals look bigger and scarier than they really are.

   _____

   _____

4. Moths have marks on their wings.

   _____

5. Fireflies beetles and bats are awake at night.

   _____

   _____

6. Ants kill spiders and insects.

   _____

7. Bats find fruit flowers and insects at night.

   _____

   _____

8. Most rain forests are filled with trees and rivers.

   _____

   _____

Elements of Literature

Use with student text page 141.

Use the Senses

Seeing 👁	Hearing 👂	Smelling 👃	Tasting 👄

➤ Write each sentence in the chart under the sense it describes.

1. My feet are wet from the rain.

2. The animals make loud noises.

3. The moths have spots on their wings.

4. The flowers smell like perfume.

5. The fireflies shine in the night.

6. I hurt my ankle walking over rocks.

7. I drink the fresh water from the river.

8. The fruit trees have a sweet smell.

9. The plants come in many sizes, shapes, and colors.

10. The fruit from the trees is sweet.

VISIONS A Activity Book • Copyright © Heinle

Word Study

Use with student text page 142.

Learn Word Roots

Sometimes words that look like other words have the same **root.** Roots are shorter words that often come from other languages.

When words share the same root, the meaning of one word connects to the other. The roots of the words in the chart come from the Latin language.

Words That Share the Same Latin Root		
Word	**Meaning**	**Part of Speech**
prey	an animal hunted by other animals for food	noun
predators	animals that kill other animals for food	noun
predatory	having to do with killing other animals for food	adjective

A. ➤ Complete the sentences. Use the words in the chart.

1. Many animals have to protect themselves from _____.

2. Some animals hunt for their _____ at night.

3. Many animals are _____, because they have to kill other animals to eat.

B. ➤ Write three sentences of your own. Use words from the chart.

1. _____

2. _____

3. _____

Grammar Focus

Use with student text page 142.

Identify the Subject and Verb of a Complete Sentence

A complete sentence has a **subject** (the noun or pronoun doing the action). It also has a **verb** (the word that shows the action).

Animals scare each other.

In this sentence, *animals* is the subject. *Scare* is the verb.

➤ Read each sentence. If it is a complete sentence, write the subject and the verb. If the sentence is not complete, write *not complete*.

1. Many rain forest animals.

not complete

2. Creatures protect themselves.

Subject: Creatures, Verb: protect

3. Animals eat other animals.

_____

4. Some animals hide.

_____

5. Moths with big wings.

_____

6. Many animals with large eyes.

_____

7. Big eyes let in more light.

_____

8. Bats fly in the rain forest.

_____

Name _____ Date _____

Grammar Focus

Use with student text page 142.

Learn Regular and Irregular Noun Plurals

Regular Noun Plurals

Most plural forms are made by adding *-s* to the noun. For example:

Singular (one): bat

Plural (more than one): bat**s**

Rule: Just add *-s*.

Some nouns have spelling changes. For example:

Singular: party

Plural: parties

Rule: If a word ends in *y*, and the letter before the *y* is a consonant, drop the *y* and add *-ies*.

A. ➤ Fill in the plural form and the rule for each word. The first one has been done for you.

Regular Plural Forms		
Singular	**Plural**	**What's the rule?**
1. army	**1.** armies	**1.** If a word ends in *y*, and the letter before the *y* is a consonant, drop the *y* and add *-ies*.
2. way	**2.**	**2.**
3. butterfly	**3.**	**3.**

Irregular Noun Plurals

➤ Some words have **irregular** plural forms. Look at these examples:

Irregular Plural Forms	
Singular	**Plural**
tooth	teeth
foot	feet
child	children

Irregular Plural Forms	
Singular	**Plural**
man	men
woman	women
fish	fish

B. ➤ Edit these sentences. If the sentence is correct, write *correct*. If a word or group of words is incorrect, write the correct form of the plural.

Student Handbook

1. There were many fish in the river. ___*correct*___

2. The bat has two foots and many sharp teeths. _____

3. Both mens and womens went into the forest. _____

From Reading to Writing

Use with student text page 143.

Edit an Informational Report

A. ➤ Use the checklist to edit the informational report you wrote in Chapter 5.

Editing Checklist for an Informational Report

_____ 1. I wrote the report in the third person, using *he, she, it,* and *they.*

_____ 2. I did not use the words *I* or *we* in the report.

_____ 3. I wrote complete sentences. Each sentence has a subject and a verb.

_____ 4. I wrote about a place in my town or city.

_____ 5. I separated the report into sections.

_____ 6. I gave each section a heading that showed the main idea of the section.

_____ 7. I gave my report a title.

_____ 8. I drew pictures to go with my report.

B. ➤ Write what you could have done differently or better in your report. Give at least two examples.

_____

_____

_____

_____

_____

_____

_____

_____

Name _____ Date _____

Across Content Areas

Use with student text page 143.

Use a Map

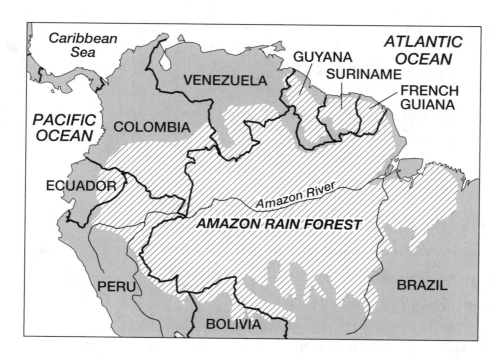

➤ Answer the questions in complete sentences. Use the map.

1. What country is most of the Amazon Rain Forest found in?

_____

2. Which river runs through the middle of the Amazon Rain Forest?

_____

3. Which ocean is next to the Amazon Rain Forest?

_____

4. Which is the smallest county shown on the map?

_____

5. Which is the largest country shown on the map?

_____

VISIONS **Unit 2 • Chapter 5** Rain Forest Creatures

VISIONS A Activity Book • Copyright © Heinle

Build Vocabulary

Use with student text page 153.

Define Words

➤ Study the words and their definitions.

> **Word and Definition**
> **shall** will
> **overcome** fight against something successfully
> **dignity** pride in oneself
> **alone** all by yourself
> **heart** deep feeling
> **believe** think; have faith in
> **marches** groups of people walking together to make a political point

A. ➤ Complete the sentences. Use the words in the box. The first one has been done for you.

1. If you __*believe*_____ you can make the world a better place, then you will.

2. When I finish school, I _____ work hard to earn a good living.

3. People walk in _____ to show support for something.

4. We all face problems in life, but we can try to _____ them.

5. You will never be _____ as long as you are a good friend to others.

6. The audience believed the speaker because he spoke with a lot of
_____.

7. People who act with _____ are treated nicely by others.

B. ➤ Underline the word that does not fit in each list.

1. shall, will, past, future

2. overcome, win, succeed, fail

3. disrespect, dignity, honor, esteem

4. one, isolated, together, alone

5. heart, emotion, feeling, head

6. trust, believe, faith, doubt

7. marches, scatter, street, walk

VISIONS Unit 3 • Chapter 1 We Shall Overcome

Writing: Capitalization and Punctuation

Use with student text page 158.

Punctuate a Song

Punctuation means commas, periods, and other writing marks. The punctuation rules for songs and poems are a little different than other writing.

Look at this example from the song "We Shall Overcome":

We shall overcome,

We shall overcome,

We shall overcome someday.

Oh, deep in my heart I do believe,

we shall overcome someday.

Notice where the commas and periods are. The commas show that a sentence goes on. The period shows that the sentence ends.

➤ Edit these sentences to look like the song. Add the missing punctuation marks. Capitalize the first letters as in the song. The first one has been done for you.

1. <u>We</u> shall walk together,

2. we shall walk together

3. we shall walk together today

4. oh deep in my heart I do believe

5. we shall walk together someday

6. i will be your friend

7. i will be your friend

8. i will be your friend today

9. oh how I wish we all were friends

10. i will be your friend today

Elements of Literature

Use with student text page 159.

Listen for Sound Devices in Music

In the song, "We Shall Overcome," there is a certain **rhythm** (a beat, like a drum). In each **stanza** (group of lines), there is the same number of syllables.

A **syllable** is a part of a word with one sound. For example:

The word *believe* has two syllables, *be-* and *-lieve*.

Count the syllables for each line as if you are clapping your hands. You would clap once for each syllable. Look at the first three lines:

clap clap clap clap clap
We shall live in peace, <5 syllables>

clap clap clap clap clap
We shall live in peace, <5 syllables >

clap clap clap clap clap clap clap
We shall live in peace someday. <7 syllables >

A. ➤ Write the number of syllables in the last two lines of the song.

1. Oh, deep in my heart I do believe, _____

2. We shall live in peace someday. _____

B. ➤ Write the number of syllables in this song lyric.

1. Down in the valley, _____

2. The valley so low, _____

3. Hang your head over, _____

4. Hear the wind blow. _____

C. ➤ Why do you think people who write songs use rhythm? Give your opinion. There is no right or wrong answer.

_____

_____

Word Study

Use with student text page 160.

Use Homophones

Homophones are words that are pronounced the same, but have different spellings and meanings.

The word *peace* and *piece* sound the same. However, *peace* means "no war," and *piece* means "one part."

➤ Study these homophones.

Homophones		
Homophone	**Meaning**	**Example**
Do	to make or prepare	*Do* your homework.
Due	when something should be finished	Your paper is *due* on Friday.
Dew	small drops of wetness from the air	In the morning, the grass was covered in *dew*.
To	preposition (part of speech) that shows direction	Let's go *to* the store.
Too	also	He likes ice cream, *too*.
Two	the number after one	I have *two* pencils.
There	shows a place or that something exists	My book is over *there*.
Their	belongs to them	*Their* books are on the table.
They're	a contraction for "they are"	*They're* from Mexico.

➤ Complete each sentence with the correct homophone. The first one has been done for you.

1. ___*Do*_____ the math problems in pencil. (Do/Due/Dew)

2. Because of the _____ outside, it looked like it rained. (do/due/dew)

3. All of our homework is _____ at 8:30 A.M. (do/due/dew)

4. Every day I eat _____ cookies. (to/too/two)

5. We study Spanish, and English, _____. (to/too/two)

6. Where do you go _____ school? (to/too/two)

7. _____ house is on the corner. (There/Their/They're)

8. _____ my neighbors. (There/Their/They're)

9. _____ is my locker. (There/Their/They're)

Grammar Focus

Use with student text page 160.

Study the Future Tense with *Will*

The **future tense** describes things that will happen in the future. Use *will* or *shall* plus a simple verb. *Will* is used much more often than *shall*.

The verb *will* can be used in a contracted (shortened) form. Study the chart.

Subject + *Will*	Contraction
I + will	I'll
you + will	you'll
we + will	we'll
they + will	they'll
he + will	he'll
she + will	she'll

➤ Rewrite the present tense sentences as future tense sentences with *will*. Add a future time expression such as *tomorrow, next week,* or *a year from now.* Then rewrite the sentence with a contraction.

1. We eat cereal for breakfast. (Use *will*)

   We will eat cereal for breakfast tomorrow morning.

   We'll eat cereal for breakfast tomorrow morning.

2. They live in California.

   _____

3. I go to school in five days.

   _____

   _____

4. I hear the song on the radio.

   _____

   _____

5. You study math.

   _____

6. You sit at the table.

   _____

   _____

Grammar Focus

Use with student text page 160.

Use Future Tense Questions and Negatives

In the future tense, use *will* plus the simple form of a verb. To ask a question, put *will* before the subject.

Future Tense Statement: She will go to the movies.

Future Tense Question: Will she go to the movies?

To answer a question in the negative, add the word *not* after *will*. The contraction for *will not* is *won't*.

She will <u>not</u> go to the movies. She <u>won't</u> go to the movies.

➤ Rewrite the sentences as questions. Then answer the question in the negative, using the word *not*. Answer it again using *won't*.

1. He will go to school tomorrow.

   Will he go to school tomorrow?

   He will not go to school tomorrow. He won't go to school tomorrow.

2. They will eat dinner at home.

   _____

   _____

3. I will paint my room.

   _____

   _____

4. She will take pictures today.

   _____

   _____

5. You will play soccer on Saturday.

   _____

   _____

Student
Handbook

From Reading to Writing

Use with student text page 161.

Edit Lyrics for a Song About the Future

➤ Use the checklist to edit the song you wrote in Chapter 1.

Editing Checklist for Lyrics for a Song About the Future

Title of song: _____

What I did:

_____ **1.** I chose a topic (a subject) for my song.

_____ **2.** My song used repetition (sounds or words used over again).

_____ **3.** I wrote my song so it could be sung in rhythm (with a beat).

_____ **4.** I used the word *will* or *shall* to show the song is in the future.

_____ **5.** I performed the song to my class.

_____ **6.** I gave my song a title.

Across Content Areas

Use with student text page 161.

Take Notes

Read this **encyclopedia** article. An encyclopedia is a book, CD-ROM, or Web site that gives information about different topics.

While you read the passage, write notes on the card about each type of song.

Types of Songs

There are many different types of songs. Each of these types of songs is sung in many languages and places.

Shanties are work songs that started in the 1800s. Workers sang them to make their work easier. They kept the workers from getting bored and tired.

Lullabies are songs that are sung to help babies fall asleep. One of the most famous lullabies is called "Hush, Little Baby."

Another type of song is an **anthem.** Anthems show respect for a country. The national anthem of the United States is called the "Star Spangled Banner." It was written by Francis Scott Key in 1814. It became the national anthem in 1931.

Ballads are songs that tell stories. They are slow and sweet in their sound, even when they are about sad stories.

Folk songs tell about things that happen every day. There may also be dances that go with the songs. Folk songs are sometimes sung by parents to their children.

Question — *What types of songs are there?*

Notes — *shanty:*

lullaby:

anthem:

ballad:

folk song:

Build Vocabulary

Use with student text page 163.

Use Antonyms

Antonyms are words that have opposite meanings. The antonym for the word *on* is *off*.

➤ Study the chart.

Vocabulary Word	Meaning	Antonym (Opposite)
inhuman	cruel	kind
parting	leaving	joining
packed	crowded	empty
whispering	talking quietly	shouting
constantly	always	never
cellar	basement	attic
brave	strong, fearless	afraid

➤ Complete the sentences. Use the vocabulary word or its antonym, depending on the meaning of the sentence. The first one has been done for you.

1. The people were very friendly and ___*kind*___. (inhuman/kind)

2. They waved good-bye as they were _____ at the airport. (parting/joining)

3. There were only one or two people, so most of the seats were _____. (packed/empty)

4. She was _____ during the movie so she would not bother other people. (whispering/shouting)

5. Gabe _____ washes the dishes, so there is a big pile in the sink. (constantly/never)

6. The food was downstairs in the _____. (cellar/attic)

7. The firefighter was very _____. She entered a burning building to save a cat. (brave/afraid)

Writing: Capitalization

Use with student text page 172.

Capitalize Names of Places

Here are some examples of places that are capitalized:

Cities: **D**allas, **N**ew **Y**ork **C**ity, **L**os **A**ngeles

States: **I**llinois, **N**ew **J**ersey, **I**daho

Countries: **V**ietnam, **M**exico, **J**apan

Continents: **E**urope, **A**sia

Also, some words that have to do with geography are capitalized, but only if they are named. For example:

Balkan **P**eninsula (but not the word *peninsula* by itself)

Atlantic **O**cean (but not the word *ocean* by itself)

Rocky **M**ountains (but not the word *mountains* by itself)

We also *sometimes* capitalize words that have to do with direction. For example:

The war between the <u>North</u> and <u>South</u> was in the 1800s.

(North and South refer to regions, or areas of land.)

but:

I live <u>south</u> of my grandparents.

(The word *south* refers to a direction. It is not capitalized.)

A. ➤ Edit this paragraph. Capitalize the letters that need to be capitalized.

The country of Bosnia and herzegovina was part of yugoslavia. It is in southeastern Europe. The capital city is called sarajevo. Bosnia is between croatia and Serbia. It is next to Montenegro. These countries are on the Balkan Peninsula on the adriatic Sea.

B. ➤ Write two sentences using names of places where you live.

1. _____

   _____

2. _____

   _____

Elements of Literature

Use with student text page 173.

Understand Point of View

The author of "Zlata's Diary," Zlata Filopović, writes from her **point of view.** Point of view is the perspective, or position, from which a story is told. In other words, Zlata writes about her own experiences, thoughts, and feelings.

"Zlata's Diary" gives us one point of view about a war. There are other points of view we can learn about. We can learn them from visuals, from other people who were there (called eyewitnesses), or from news reports.

➤ Look at these three different ways of learning about the war in Yugoslavia.

Soldiers patrol the city.

World Report

Dobrinja is destroyed.
Residents left homeless.

Eyewitness Report:

"In the middle of the town, it is quiet. It was a warm spring day today. We went outside. The streets were full of people."

➤ Write what you learned about the war.

1. From the photograph, I learned:

_____

_____

2. From the newspaper report, I learned:

_____

_____

3. From the eyewitness account, I learned:

_____

_____

4. Why is it important to have more than one way to get information?

_____

_____

Word Study

Use with student text page 174.

Use Contractions

Contractions are used to make words shorter. They are formed by joining two words together. Letters are dropped and replaced by an apostrophe (').

we + are = we're

The apostrophe takes the place of the letter *a*.

Contractions Using the Verb *To Be*	
Subject + Verb	**Contraction**
I am	I'm
You are	You're
He is	He's
She is	She's
It is	It's
We are	We're
They are	They're

A. ➤ Answer the questions. Use contractions from the chart.

1. What are you doing now? _____

2. Where is your teacher? _____

3. Where are your shoes? _____

4. What are you studying? _____

5. What is your favorite sport? _____

6. Where is your school? _____

7. What TV programs do you and your family watch? _____

8. What is your mother cooking? _____

B. ➤ Complete the sentences with contractions from the chart.

1. My brother and I are going to the soccer game tomorrow. _____ happy about that.

2. Mr. Roberts is the coach. _____ strict, but _____ very good.

3. The students need to hurry. _____ late for class.

4. I didn't do my homework. _____ in trouble!

Grammar Focus

Use with student text page 174.

Use Verbs with Infinitives

The infinitive form of a verb is the word *to* plus the simple form of the verb.

<u>to</u> run

<u>to</u> sing

<u>to</u> play

A. ➤ Underline the infinitive verb in each sentence. If there is no infinitive, write *none*.

1. I don't think they know what <u>to do</u>.

2. I talked on the phone with my friend.

3. She had to go back to the house.

4. Verica plans to go away.

Some verbs can be followed by infinitives. Here are some of them.

want	promise	decide
need	try	like

I **wanted to help** the little kids.

B. ➤ Complete the sentences with infinitives from the box.

to play	to buy
to listen	to write
to go	to move
to meet	

1. They decided _____ to the movies.

2. The kids want _____ soccer, not baseball.

3. I'm going to make an apple pie, but I need _____ some apples.

4. I have to go. I promised _____ my little brother at the bus stop.

5. I like _____ to music while I work.

6. We decided _____ our report on the Balkan Peninsula.

Grammar Focus

Use with student text page 174.

Use Infinitives

➤ Edit these sentences. Look at each underlined verb form and decide if it is correct. If the sentence is incorrect, rewrite it. If there are no mistakes, write *correct*.

1. I need <u>buy</u> some milk.

I need to buy some milk.

2. We need <u>to go</u> to the store.

_____

3. She promised <u>to cleans</u> her room.

_____

4. They need <u>ask</u> a question.

_____

5. You should try <u>get</u> along.

_____

6. Do you want <u>decide</u> today?

_____

7. He wants <u>to learn</u> how to dance.

_____

8. I hope <u>to visit</u> you soon.

_____

9. We want <u>begin</u> at 7:00 A.M.

_____

10. Have you ever tried <u>swim</u>?

_____

Student
Handbook

From Reading to Writing

Use with student text page 175.

Edit an Opinion

A. ➤ Use the checklist to edit the opinion you wrote in Chapter 2.

Editing Checklist for Writing an Opinion

What I did:

_____ **1.** I wrote my opinion in the topic (first) sentence.

_____ **2.** I indented my paragraph.

_____ **3.** I used details to support my opinion.

_____ **4.** I used correct capitalization for names of people and places.

_____ **5.** I used correct punctuation at the ends of sentences.

_____ **6.** I used contractions correctly.

B. ➤ What could you have done differently when you wrote your opinion? What could be changed to make it better?

_____

_____

_____

_____

_____

_____

_____

Across Content Areas

Use with student text page 175.

Use Map Skills

Maps give us many different kinds of information. They show us:

continents (large pieces of land)

oceans and seas (large areas of water)

cities (marked with a circle or with a star if they are capital cities)

countries (places that are larger than cities and smaller than continents)

directions, using a compass (north, south, east, and west)

➤ Study this map of southeast Europe. Underline the correct answers. Use the map to help you.

1. Europe is (a continent/an ocean).

2. Croatia is (a city/a country).

3. A compass rose tells (north, south, east, and west/how far it takes to get someplace).

4. The Adriatic is (a sea/an ocean).

5. The Ionian Sea is (north/south) of Italy.

6. Slovenia is (a country/a continent).

7. This map (shows/does not show) mountains.

8. Bosnia-Herzegovina (has/does not have) water on one side.

9. Serbia (is/is not) in Bosnia.

10. Croatia is (north/south) of Bosnia-Herzegovina.

Build Vocabulary

Use with student text page 177.

Put Words Into a Group and Understand Syllables

Putting words into groups can help you understand the words' meanings. For example:

A peach is a kind of <u>fruit</u>.

An apple is a <u>fruit</u>.

An apple and a peach are words that belong in a group called *fruits*.

A. ➤ Fill in the chart. Use the words in the box.

	Tree Words	**Water Words**
1. scrub (wash)		
2. firewood		
3. floating (staying up in water)		
4. stick		
5. island (land that has water all around it)		
6. sea		
7. boat		

B. ➤ Read the definitions of words that show movement. Underline the kind of animal they go with. (A pheasant is a colorful bird with a long tail.)

1. **slink** walk as if afraid or guilty (dog/pheasant/monkey)

2. **peck** hit with a sharp object, such as a bird's beak (dog/pheasant/monkey)

3. **climb** move up (dog/pheasant/monkey)

4. **leap** jump (dog/pheasant/monkey)

5. **fly** move through the air (dog/pheasant/monkey)

Writing: Punctuation

Use with student text page 186.

Use Exclamation Points

An exclamation point ends a sentence that expresses strong emotion. Look at the examples:

This is my lucky day**!**

What a fine big peach this is**!**

Look at this peach**!**

A. ➤ Add the final punctuation. Write a period if the sentence just gives information. Write an exclamation point if the sentence shows strong emotion.

1. Wow, I won the race__!__

2. Today, I ate a sandwich for lunch___

3. Look, there is a boy inside the peach___

4. Oh no___

5. I will be back soon___

6. Help me, I'm falling___

7. I would like to go with you to the mall___

8. Come here right now___

9. I got an A on my test___

10. There were a few good books___

B. ➤ Write three sentences with exclamation points.

1. _____

2. _____

3. _____

Elements of Literature

Use with student text page 187.

Recognize Problems and Resolutions

Many stories like "The Peach Boy" have problems and **resolutions** (ways the problems are solved).

Problem: The old man and old woman had no children.

Resolution: One day, they found a boy inside a peach.

A. ➤ Match the problems to their resolutions.

Problems

_____c_____ 1. It starts to rain.

_____ 2. He is late for the school bus.

_____ 3. He leaves his book at school.

_____ 4. She is hungry.

_____ 5. She is lost.

_____ 6. He is cold.

_____ 7. She is thirsty.

_____ 8. He needs help with English.

_____ 9. She is tired.

_____ 10. He needs a pencil.

Resolutions

a. He returns to school to get it.

b. She gets a drink of water.

c. She takes out an umbrella.

d. He puts on a sweater.

e. She eats lunch.

f. She asks for directions.

g. He runs so he will not miss it.

h. She goes to bed.

i. He asks the teacher for help.

j. A friend gives him one.

B. ➤ Think of a story you have read. Answer the questions.

1. What was the problem in the story?

_____

_____

_____

2. What was the resolution?

_____

_____

_____

Word Study

Use with student text page 188.

Use Synonyms to Define Words

Words that have similar meanings are called **synonyms.** For example, *unhappy* and *sad* are synonyms.

Study the list of words and synonyms. These words are adjectives that describe feelings.

Adjective	Synonym
fine	good
wonderful	excellent
fortunate	lucky
delighted	happy
appreciative	thankful

A. ➤ Complete the sentences. Use the *adjectives* in the chart.

1. The man thought the peach would make a ___wonderful___ dinner.

2. The man and the woman were _____ that they finally had a child.

3. Momotaro was _____ of the dog's offer to help.

4. The woman said, "This is my lucky day!" She was _____ to have found the peach.

5. It was a _____ thing to find the peach. The woman felt good about it.

B. ➤ Write five sentences about yourself. Use the *synonyms* in the chart. The first one has been done for you.

1. *I did a good job cleaning my room.* _____

2. _____

3. _____

4. _____

5. _____

Grammar Focus

Use with student text page 188.

Use Compound Sentences with *And*

A **compound sentence** joins two complete sentences together.

When compound sentences are joined with *and*, use a comma before the word *and*. There is no capital letter at the beginning of the second part of the sentence.

Two complete sentences: He went up to bat. He got a hit.

Compound sentence: He went up to bat, and he got a hit.

Notice the comma and the word *and*. Notice the word *he* is not capitalized.

➤ Rewrite the sentences by joining them together. The first one has been done for you.

1. An old man and an old woman lived in a village in Japan.
   They had no children.

   An old man and an old woman lived in a village in Japan, and they had no children.

2. The woman went to wash clothes.
   The man went to cut some firewood.

   _____

3. The mother made some cakes.
   The boy took them.

   _____

4. Momotaro was walking.
   He saw a monkey.

   _____

5. They came to the sea.
   Momotaro found a boat.

   _____

6. Momotaro met the dog.
   The dog said he would help.

   _____

Name _____ Date _____

Grammar Focus

Use with student text page 188.

Use Compound Sentences

Remember, when joining two sentences, you must use a comma after the first sentence. For example:

We found jewels, and we found other fine goods.

You do not need to use a comma before every *and*. You only use a comma if you are joining two complete sentences with two subjects and two verbs. For example:

I ate apples and drank orange juice.

There is no comma. The sentence has two verbs (*ate* and *drank*) but only one subject (*I*).

➤ Edit these sentences. Rewrite the sentences by adding the missing comma. If the sentence is correct, write *correct*.

1. He returned home and he was happy.

   He returned home, and he was happy.
   _____

2. Momotaro returned the stolen goods and he told the people not to worry.

   _____

3. He will fly over the gate and peck at the ogres!

   _____

4. The monkey climbed over the wall and he pinched the ogres.

   _____

5. I would like to go with you and I think I can help you.

   _____

6. There were many treasures and jewels left.

   _____

7. The dog and I will help.

   _____

Student
Handbook

From Reading to Writing

Use with student text page 189.

Write a Summary

A **summary** gives the most important ideas of a text or part of a text. For example:

The sun was shining. I went to the river and caught ten fish. Then I went home and read a book. That night, I cooked a great dinner.

The summary for this text might be:

I had a nice day. I did what I wanted and had a good time.

➤ Fill in the paragraph guide to help you write your summary. Think about the most important parts in the play. Write at least two sentences for each part.

○ *"The Peach Boy" is about* _____

_____

_____.

One day, _____

_____

○ _____.

Years later, _____

_____

_____.

At the end of the play, _____

○ _____

_____.

Name _____ Date _____

Across Content Areas

Use with student text page 189.

Classify Fruits and Vegetables

There are many ways to classify (group) things. Look at the list of fruits and vegetables.

carrot	watermelon	spinach
apple	banana	lemon
tomato	strawberry	peas
pepper	cucumber	corn
orange	peach	cherries
lettuce	broccoli	celery

➤ Fill in the charts. Use the list of fruits and vegetables.

Fruits and Vegetables Classified by Color			
Red	**Yellow**	**Green**	**Orange**

Fruits and Vegetables Classified by Likes and Dislikes	
Which Ones I Like	**Which Ones I Do Not Like**

Build Vocabulary

Use with student text page 191.

Use Synonyms to Find Meaning

Synonyms are words that have similar meanings. Synonyms can sometimes help you understand other words in a sentence.

I was completely <u>delighted</u>. I had never felt so <u>happy</u> in my life.

The words *delighted* and *happy* are synonyms. If you know the meaning of one of these words, you can guess the meaning of the other.

Read these words and definitions.

Word and Definition

slope a surface at an upward or downward angle

escape get away

dishes things used to serve and hold food

dense crowded together

worried feeling that something bad might happen

sorrow sadness

trust believe, feel that someone is honest

cracked broke apart with force

➤ Replace each underlined word or phrase with a word from the box that means about the same thing.

1. The side lawn dipped at an <u>angle</u>. *slope* _____

2. They could not <u>get away</u> because the door was locked. _____

3. We had plenty of <u>plates and bowls</u>, but we had no forks or spoons.

   _____

4. The bushes were so <u>thick</u> that we couldn't get through them. _____

5. She was a little <u>scared</u> as she walked into the principal's office. _____

6. I felt deep <u>sadness</u> for the family because their house burned down.

   _____

7. I usually <u>have confidence in</u> people who tell the truth. _____

8. My voice <u>broke</u> as I yelled back at my brother. _____

Writing: Spelling

Use with student text page 202.

Spell Words with the *sh* and *ch* Sound

The *sh* Sound

The *sh* sound is written in different ways.

A. ➤ Underline the *sh* sound in the following words.

1. action   3. sure

2. shadow   4. possession

Words with the Letters *sh*	Letters That Make the *sh* Sound
di<u>sh</u>es	sh
auc<u>ti</u>on	ti
in<u>s</u>urance <u>s</u>ure	s (sometimes after *u*)
mi<u>ssi</u>on	ssi

B. ➤ Underline the words that have the *sh* sound.

1. shout   brush   church

2. education   educate   brushes

3. sure   shine   session

The *ch* Sound

The *ch* sound is also written in different ways.

C. ➤ Underline the *ch* sound in the following words.

1. clutched   3. situation

2. porch   4. teacher

Words with the Letters *ch*	Letters That Make the *ch* Sound
kit<u>ch</u>en	*ch*
furni<u>tu</u>re	*tu*

D. ➤ Each of these words has either the *sh* or *ch* sound. Underline the words that make the sound, and write *sh* or *ch* in the blank.

1. chicken _____

2. sugar _____

3. tradition _____

4. much _____

5. picture _____

Elements of Literature

Use with student text page 203.

Analyze Character Traits, Motivations, and Points of View

Authors use different techniques to describe characters.

- **Traits** describe how characters look and behave.
- **Motivation** describes why characters do things.
- **Point of view** or **perspective** shows the character's opinions, likes, and dislikes.

➤ Write which technique is used in each sentence. Use the techniques in the box. The first one has been done for you.

1. I could crawl between the bushes and hide from my brother. It was quiet and beautiful there. ___motivation___

2. I was mostly wild and joyful. _____

3. He expected me to drop everything and come to help him. _____

4. My father made me speak to the lady on the phone because he could not speak English. _____

5. I hated talking to people on the phone. When my father called me, I wished I could have escaped. _____

6. The lady was slim with smooth dark hair. _____

7. I think she is wasting her time. _____

8. She said that she came to ask for the dishes because they belonged to her grandmother and they have special meaning for her. _____

9. My father was a small man but he looked scary at times. _____

10. Tell her that I am certain that the dishes belong to us. They were in the house when we moved in. _____

11. The lady appeared to be a bit worried. _____

12. I returned the dishes to her because we did not need them. _____

Word Study

Use with student text page 204.

Use the Prefix *dis-*

A **prefix** is a group of letters added to the beginning of a word. A prefix can change the meaning of a word.

When the prefix *dis-* is added to a word, the new word often changes to mean the opposite thing. For example, *connect* means "to join together." *Disconnect* means "to pull apart."

A. ➤ Fill in the chart. The first one has been done for you.

Word	Meaning	New Word *Dis-* + Word	New Meaning
approve	agree with	disapprove	not agree with
contented	happy		
honest	telling the truth		
like	enjoy		
order	organization		
obey	follow rules		
prove	show to be true		
comfort	ease, without pain		

B. ➤ Complete the sentences. Use the new words in the chart.

1. After one week in the hospital, she still felt __*discomfort*__ from the surgery.

2. I _____ being out in large crowds. I would rather stay home and read.

3. We knew she was being _____. She looks down when she is lying.

4. Your desk is in complete _____. It is a total mess!

5. Most teachers _____ of students who chew gum in school.

6. Sometimes, students who _____ school rules have to stay after school.

7. In our science experiment, we may _____ the theory.

8. He never smiles. He always seems _____.

VISIONS A Activity Book • Copyright © Heinle

Grammar Focus

Use with student text page 204.

Use *Could* with Statements and Questions

Use *Could* with Statements

Could is the past of *can*. Use *could* with the simple form of a verb to describe actions that the subject was able to do in the past.

Joe <u>could</u> run five miles.

Joe didn't get good grades at school. His parents made some new rules for him. He started following the rules today.

Rules for Joe

No TV on school nights.
No telephone calls on school nights.
No trips to the mall on Saturday.

Use the computer only for homework—
    NOT for games.
Be in bed by 10:00 every night.

A. ➤ Complete these sentences using *could* and the verbs in parentheses.

1. Yesterday, Joe _*could watch*_____ (watch) TV on school nights, but today he can't.

2. Yesterday, Joe _____ (talk) on the phone on school nights, but now he can't.

3. Last week, he _____ (go) to the mall on Saturday, but this week he can't.

4. Yesterday, he _____ (play) games on the computer, but today he can't.

5. Last night, he _____ (stay up) late, but tonight he can't.

Use *Could* with Questions

Form questions with *could* by putting *could* before the subject.

<u>Could</u> Joe talk on the phone on school nights yesterday?

B. ➤ Write three questions about what Joe could do before he had the new rules.

1. _____

2. _____

3. _____

Name _____ Date _____

Grammar Focus

Use with student text page 204.

Use the Negative Form of *Could* with Statements

To make a negative statement with *could,* put *not* after *could.* The contracted form (shortened form) of *could not* is *couldn't.*

Isabel <u>could not</u> wait to see her grandmother.

Isabel <u>couldn't</u> wait to see her grandmother.

A. ➤ Answer each question by using *could not.* Then rewrite it using *couldn't.*

1. Could you play tennis?

No, <u>*I could not play tennis*</u> _____ because I did not have a tennis racquet.

No, <u>*I couldn't play tennis*</u> _____ because I did not have a tennis racquet.

2. Could he walk to school?

No, _____ because he didn't live nearby.

No, _____ because he didn't live nearby.

3. Could we read the book?

No, _____ because they didn't know Chinese.

No, _____ because they didn't know Chinese.

4. Could they run fast?

No, _____ because they didn't have good running shoes.

No, _____ because they didn't have good running shoes.

5. Could you and the children play outside?

No, _____ because it was too cold.

No, _____ because it was too cold.

B. ➤ Write three sentences about what you *couldn't* do at some time in the past. Use a clause with *because* to give a reason why you couldn't do it.

1. _____

2. _____

3. _____

Student
Handbook

From Reading to Writing

Use with student text page 205.

Edit a Response to Literature

➤ Use the checklist to edit the paragraph you wrote in Chapter 4.

Editing Checklist for Response to Literature

_____ **1.** I chose an ending for the story.

_____ **2.** I used at least two reasons to explain the character's motivation.

_____ **3.** I wrote the paragraph from Edite's point of view using the pronouns *I, me, we,* and *us.*

_____ **4.** I indented my paragraph.

_____ **5.** I capitalized the names of the characters in the story.

_____ **6.** I used punctuation marks correctly.

Across Content Areas

Use with student text page 205.

Edit Using Graphic Features

Graphic features are used to help readers organize and identify important information. Look at this list of graphic features:

Graphic Features		
Feature	**Description**	**Uses**
Boldface Type	Darker type that looks like this: **boldface**	Important words
Italic Type	Slanted letters that look like this: *italic*	Titles of books Words from other languages
Bullets	Dots like this: •	Items in a list

A. ➤ Read the paragraphs. Underline words you think should be in *italic* type. Underline with two lines words you think should be in **boldface** type. Circle words you think should be in a list with bullets.

Portugal

Portugal is a country in the Iberian Peninsula, in southwest Europe. It became independent in 1143. Portugal's capital is Lisbon, a port city on the Atlantic Ocean.

Many past explorers came from Portugal. One explorer was Vasco da Gama. He found a sea route around Africa and into the Indian Ocean. Many books about him have been published, including, *The Diary of the First Voyage of Vasco da Gama.*

Portugal has about 20 inches (50 cm) of rainfall each year. Because of the rain, there is a lot of farming in Portugal. Some agricultural products grown in Portugal are:

wheat

corn

barley

olives

grapes

cork

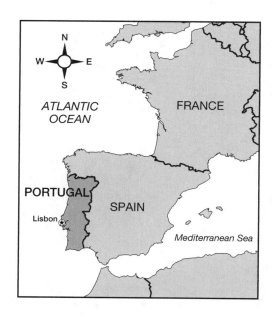

Build Vocabulary

Use with student text page 207.

Identify Analogies

An **analogy** is a type of comparison. An analogy often shows how two situations are similar. Here is an example of an analogy:

<u>elephant is to large</u> as <u>ant is to small</u>

This example shows a relationship between the sizes of two different living things. The analogy is another way of saying, "an elephant is very large and an ant is very small."

Word and Definition

flavor an exciting quality

prevent stop from happening

frown to show anger or sadness with the mouth and eyes

tranquility peace, calmness

confrontation the act of facing something difficult or dangerous

psychiatrist a doctor who treats mental problems

volunteer when people help other people for no pay

➤ Complete the analogies. Use the words and definitions in the box to help you.

Analogies

1. dull is to boring as flavor is to _<u>b</u>_
   a. flat   **b.** interesting   **c.** wonderful   **d.** empty

2. allow is to continue as prevent is to _____
   a. go   **b.** repeat   **c.** stop   **d.** produce

3. stomp is to foot as frown is to _____
   a. neck   **b.** leg   **c.** hand   **d.** face

4. tranquility is to peaceful as turmoil is to _____
   a. trouble   **b.** calm   **c.** still   **d.** ordered

5. escape is to run as confrontation is to _____
   a. meet   **b.** release   **c.** ignore   **d.** neglect

6. dentist is to teeth as psychiatrist is to _____
   a. skin   **b.** heart   **c.** bones   **d.** mind

7. employee is to salary as volunteer is to _____
   a. expensive   **b.** no pay   **c.** union   **d.** work

Writing: Spelling

Use with student text page 218.

Spell Words Ending in *-ity*

Some adjectives become nouns when *-ity* is added to the ends of them. For example, *tranquil* (peaceful and quiet) becomes *tranquility* (the state of being peaceful and quiet).

If the adjective ends in an *e*, drop the *e* before adding *-ity*. *Scarce* becomes *scarcity*.

➤ Complete the sentences by changing the adjectives into nouns.

1. She has an __*opportunity*__ (opportune) to participate in the club.

2. They have an after-school _____ (active) on Wednesdays.

3. The _____ (tranquil) of the beach helped me to relax.

4. When you are stressed, your _____ (productive) is affected.

5. Psychologists have much _____ (familiar) with the topic of stress.

6. In _____ (real), most people will have stress sometime in their life.

7. The _____ (major) of people do not let stress get out of hand.

8. Taking care of yourself is a _____ (prior).

9. Counselors can help people deal with stress with _____ (mature).

Elements of Literature

Use with student text page 219.

Organize Important Details

Many authors of informational text organize important details into sections. These sections often have titles called **headings.** Headings provide clues about important ideas in text. Read this heading:

How to Volunteer in Your Community

A writer would write information in this section that supports the main idea in the heading. For example, a writer might include information about working at a soup kitchen, visiting older citizens, and so on.

A. ➤ Fill in the chart. Use the list of details.

1. talking to a counselor
2. exercising or physical activity
3. natural disasters
4. sleep
5. following a routine

6. eating healthy foods
7. war
8. participating in school activities
9. moving away
10. having too much to do

Things That Cause Stress	Things That Lower Stress

B. ➤ Underline the detail that does not fit the heading.

Headings	Details
1. **What to Do on a Rainy Day**	read a book, listen to music, garden, cook
2. **Animals of the Desert**	snakes, fish, lizards, coyotes
3. **Types of Music**	poetry, classical, jazz, rock and roll
4. **Water Sports**	water-skiing, swimming, baseball, boating

Word Study

Use with student text page 220.

Study Words That Come from Greek

Many English words come from other languages. The language a word comes from is called its **origin.** The meanings of the English words and the words in other languages are often related.

Study the dictionary entry. Notice how the meaning of the Greek words relate to the meaning of the English word, biography.

biography /bī og´ re fē/ *noun* the story of a person's life: *He read a biography of a baseball hero.* [Greek *bios* life + *graphein* write, draw, or describe] — origin

➤ Fill in the chart. Use the meanings in the box and of the Greek words to help you.

English Word	Meaning of English Word	Greek Word	Meaning of Greek Word
telephone		tele, phone	far way, voice, sound
astronaut		aster, nautes	star sailor
graph		graphein	write, draw, or describe
biome		bios	life
phrase		phrasis	speech

Meanings of English Words
1. a group of words
2. a place that can support different forms of life
3. a person who travels into outer space
4. a machine used to communicate with the voice
5. a drawing that shows changes in quantity

Grammar Focus

Use with student text page 220.

Use Complex Sentences with *If*

A complex sentence contains an **independent clause** and one or more **dependent clauses.** A **clause** is a group of words that has a subject and verb.

An independent clause can stand alone as a complete sentence. However, a dependent clause is not a complete sentence. It cannot stand alone. It must be used with an independent clause.

Some dependent clauses begin with the word *if.* When a dependent clause with *if* begins a sentence, place a **comma (,)** after it.

Dependent Clause   Independent Clause

If you do not sleep, you will feel more stress.

Independent Clause   Dependent Clause

You will feel more stress if you do not sleep.

A. ➤ Identify the underlined clause. Write *independent* or *dependent*. The first one has been done for you.

1. If she cares, <u>she will call</u>. *independent*

2. Your mother will help you <u>if you ask her</u>. _____

3. <u>If you saw it</u>, you would understand what I mean. _____

4. <u>You will learn Spanish faster</u> if you live in Spain. _____

B. ➤ Write complex sentences by joining the clauses. Add the word *if* to the first clause.

1. You have too much stress. You can get sick.
   If you have too much stress, you can get sick.

2. We exercise. We can reduce stress.
   _____

3. You are nervous. You should exercise.
   _____

4. A problem is beyond your control. Ask for help.
   _____

Grammar Focus

Use with student text page 220.

Edit Complex Sentences

You learned:

1. An independent clause can stand alone.

2. A dependent clause cannot stand alone as a sentence. It must be used with an independent clause.

3. You use a comma after a dependent clause if it comes first in a sentence.

A. ➤ Edit the paragraph. Rewrite the sentences to show correct use of dependent and independent clauses.

If you feel angry or sad. You may be under stress. If you get sick often stress may be the cause. If you feel a lot of tension talk to a psychologist. You will feel less stress, if you take care of yourself. Get enough sleep and eat right. You will improve the quality of your life, if you do these things.

_____

_____

_____

_____

_____

_____

B. ➤ Complete each sentence with an independent clause.

1. If you practice every day, _____.

2. If everyone uses less gas, _____.

3. _____ if I want to relax.

Student
Handbook

From Reading to Writing

Use with student text page 221.

Edit Informational Text

➤ Use the checklist to edit the paragraphs you wrote in Chapter 5.

Editing Checklist for Informational Text

Title of informational text: _____

What I did:

_____ 1. I wrote an introduction that includes a thesis statement.

_____ 2. I wrote a body that includes supporting details.

_____ 3. I wrote a conclusion that explains how my ideas can help people.

_____ 4. I used the pronoun *you* to speak directly to readers.

_____ 5. I used dictionary and grammar guides to help me with spelling and writing complete sentences.

_____ 6. I cited resources I used from researching information.

Across Content Areas

Use with student text page 221.

Rank Important Information

Imagine that a journalist interviewed a group of psychologists about stress in the lives of teenagers. The journalist organized the results of the interviews into ranking ladders.

The ranking ladders are organized from greatest to least. The top rung shows the greatest of something. The bottom rung shows the least of something.

Causes of Teenage Stress
tests and grades
homework
peer problems
family problems
sports competitions

Best Ways to Cope with Teenage Stress
talk to a friend
get more sleep
exercise
join a club
listen to music

➤ Answer the questions. Use the ranking ladders.

1. What causes the greatest amount of stress among teenagers?

   _____

2. What causes the least amount of stress among teenagers?

   _____

3. What is the most effective way for teenagers to cope with stress?

   _____

4. What is the least effective way for teenagers to cope with stress?

   _____

5. Suppose you made the same ranking ladders for stress in your life. What would you write for the top and bottom parts of each ladder?

   _____

   _____

Build Vocabulary

Use with student text page 231.

Use Definitions and Alphabetize

Define Words

➤ **A.** Rewrite each sentence. Replace the underlined word with a word in the box.

Word and Definition
frail weak
farewell good-bye
loom a machine for weaving thread into cloth
fierce violent and cruel
summoned called for or sent for
harsh rough
rank a position in the army
escort guide

1. The wind was <u>strong</u>. We wore heavy scarves and hats.

    The wind was fierce. We wore extra

    scarves and hats.

2. The weaver pulled out her best <u>machine</u> to use with the beautiful wool.

    _____

3. We asked a person to <u>guide</u> us through the Rocky Mountains.

    _____

4. After being at camp with my friend, it was hard to say <u>good-bye</u> to her.

    _____

5. Chicken soup can help a <u>weak</u> person feel stronger.

    _____

6. Sometimes we have to speak in a <u>rough</u> voice to get our dog to listen to us.

    _____

7. Janice was promoted to a higher <u>position</u> in her office.

    _____

8. Mrs. Garrity <u>called for</u> Ellen.

    _____

Writing: Spelling

Use with student text page 238.

Use Silent *k* in *kn*

Silent letters are letters that are not heard when a word is pronounced.

She <u>knew</u> her father was safe.

Her brother sharpened his <u>knife</u> to prepare a pig and sheep for the feast in Mulan's honor.

The *k* in the words *knowing* and *knife* is not heard when the words are pronounced.

➤ **A.** Underline the word in each sentence with the silent *k*.

1. Mulan bent down on one knee.

2. Mulan's brother used his knife to prepare the meal.

3. Mulan's mother knit sweaters.

4. Mulan feared soldiers knocking at the door asking for her father.

5. Mulan wore her hair in a braid with a knot at the end.

6. The other soldiers did not know that Mulan was a girl.

➤ **B.** Edit these sentences. Write the words with a silent *k* correctly.

1. Greg had to nock on Jim's door, because the doorbell was broken.

_____

2. I now the answer.

_____

3. I hurt my nee when I fell.

_____

4. Teresa loves to nit with blue and green yarn.

_____

5. Be sure you tie a not that will stay tight.

_____

6. When I eat, I use a fork and a nife.

_____

Elements of Literature

Use with student text page 239.

Understand Minor Characters

The **main character** is the most important character in a story. The story focuses on the feelings and actions of that character. **Minor characters** are less important. They are involved in fewer events, but they often help the reader understand the main character.

➤ Identify the minor character in each passage. Explain how the minor character helps the reader understand the major character.

1. Her mother asked her again and again, until Mulan finally said, "There is news of war."
   The minor character is Mulan's mother. Her action shows that Mulan does not really want to say a war is coming.

2. Mulan thought she heard her mother calling her name. But it was only the sound of the river crying.

   _____

   _____

3. The Emperor summoned Mulan to the High Palace. He praised her for her bravery and leadership in battle.

   _____

   _____

4. Waiting at home, Mulan's sister beautified herself. Her brother sharpened his knife to prepare a pig and sheep for the feast in Mulan's honor.

   _____

   _____

5. Holding each other, Mulan's proud parents walked to the village gate to welcome her.

   _____

   _____

6. Mulan's comrades were astonished and amazed. "How is this possible?" they asked. "How could we have fought side by side with you for ten years and not known you were a woman!"

   _____

   _____

Word Study

Use with student text page 240.

Use the Suffix -ly to Form Adverbs

A **verb** is a word that shows action. An **adverb** describes an action. It can show *how* an action is done. For example, if you paint *neatly,* the word *neatly* shows how you paint. Many adverbs are formed by adding *-ly* to an adjective.

Adjective   Adverb

quick + *-ly* → quickly

Adverbs are very helpful in writing. They help readers form pictures of the actions in their minds.

➤ **A.** Fill in the chart. Form adverbs using *-ly.*

➤ **B.** Rewrite the sentences. Change each underlined word to one of the adverbs in the chart.

Adjective	+ -ly	Adverb
1. nice		1. nicely
2. bad		2.
3. clear		3.
4. usual	+ -ly	4.
5. sharp		5.
6. poor		6.
7. close		7.
8. loud		8.

1. The barber cut your hair very <u>nice</u>.

   The barber cut your hair very nicely.

2. Jonah fell and hurt his knee <u>bad</u>.

   _____

3. Sonja sang her part in the choir <u>clear</u>.

   _____

4. Grandia <u>usual</u> leaves her house keys in her coat.

   _____

5. Once in a while, I have to speak <u>sharp</u> to my dog.

   _____

6. I am doing <u>poor</u> with my flute lessons.

   _____

7. In soccer, Larry and Peter are <u>close</u> matched.

   _____

8. Molly said her lines <u>loud</u>.

   _____

Name _____ Date _____

Grammar Focus

Use with student text page 240.

Use Prepositional Phrases

A **preposition** is a word like *in, on,* and *under.* A **prepositional phrase** is a group of words that starts with a preposition. A prepositional phrase always includes at least one noun or pronoun. Prepositional phrases can answer the questions *where, when,* and *how.*

Where was Mulan? She was **on her horse.**

How did she fight? She fought **with her sword.**

When did the battle take place? It took place **in the winter.**

➤ **A.** Complete the sentences with a prepositional phrase from the box.

at dawn	into her bedroom	in China
with great happiness	in the market	with success
to the high palace	at the end	at the door

Mulan lived in a village _____. When war came, she went _____ to buy a horse. The next day _____, she left. For ten

1
2
3
years, she fought _____. She became a great general, but no one knew

4
that she was a woman. _____ of the war, the emperor asked her to come

5
_____. She said, "I want only a swift camel to take me home." When she

6
got home, she went _____. _____, she put on a beautiful

7
8
dress. When she appeared _____, her comrades were very surprised.

9

➤ **B.** Complete the chart below. Put the prepositional phrases from the box in Activity A into the correct columns.

"When" Prepositional Phrases	"Where" Prepositional Phrases	"How" Prepositional Phrases
at dawn		

Name _____ Date _____

Grammar Focus

Use with student text page 240.

Find the Object of the Preposition

The noun or pronoun in a prepositional phrase is the **object of the preposition.**

Preposition   Object of the Preposition

The cat is under the table.

Prepositional Phrase

➤ Underline the prepositional phrases in these sentences. Circle the objects of prepositions. Some sentences have more than one prepositional phrase.

1. I do not know much about this town.

   town _____

2. I heard about it before the holidays.

   _____

3. I have some nice neighbors who live down the street.

   _____

4. Some of my cousins live near me.

   _____

5. My cousin Sheila is inside her house.

   _____

6. She is the only girl except me who lives in our neighborhood.

   _____

7. Two of my classmates live on my block.

   _____

8. They walk to school with me.

   _____

Student
Handbook

VISIONS A Activity Book • Copyright © Heinle

Name _____ Date _____

From Reading to Writing

Use with student text page 241.

Prewrite for a Legend

Legends are made-up stories that have been passed down from generation to generation. They are about people who do great things. These people are often called **heroes** or **heroines.**

➤ **A.** Think about a hero or heroine from a legend. Write the person's name in the center oval. Fill in the word web with words that describe what special things the person has done.

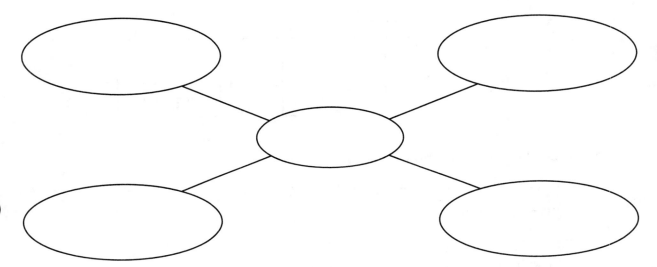

➤ **B.** Write sentences to use as notes for your legend. Use the information from your word web. You may exaggerate to make your legend more exciting.

Across Content Areas

Use with student text page 241.

Read a Flowchart

A **flowchart** is a visual guide. It shows steps in a process. Use a flowchart to visualize and remember the order and steps in a process. Study the flowchart. Answer the questions.

How Green Tea Is Made

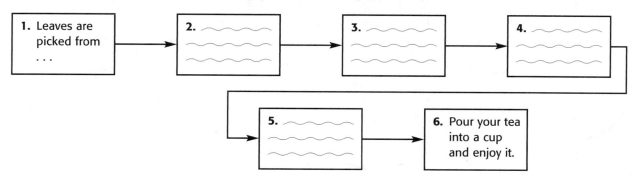

1. What does the flowchart show?

_____

2. How many steps are in the process?

_____

3. Draw a flowchart for one of these processes. Write the steps.

   • how to make coffee

   • how to make orange juice

VISIONS Unit 4 • Chapter 1 The Ballad of Mulan

VISIONS A Activity Book • Copyright © Heinle

Build Vocabulary

Use with student text page 243.

Find Synonyms

Words that have similar meanings are called **synonyms.** Use a dictionary if you need help.

➤ **A.** Match the underlined word in each sentence to its synonym.

Word in a Sentence

1. ___*b*___ Families from other countries are proud of their <u>heritage</u>.

2. _____ Winners of Olympic events are <u>awarded</u> gold medals.

3. _____ Jon's family <u>begged</u> him to stay home during the snowstorm.

4. _____ <u>Unfortunately</u>, many people died in an earthquake a few years ago.

5. _____ It is very <u>tragic</u> when an accident happens that kills many people.

6. _____ A person who is a <u>humanitarian</u> makes the world a better place.

7. _____ My grandfather is <u>proud</u> of where he came from.

Synonym

a. urged

b. traditions

c. sad

d. helper

e. given

f. sadly

g. satisfied

➤ **B.** Choose three of the words or synonyms and use them in sentences of your own.

1. _____

2. _____

3. _____

Writing: Capitalization

Use with student text page 248.

Capitalize Names and Places

Proper nouns are words that name specific people, places, and things. They are always capitalized.

Roberto **C**lemente **W**alker was born in **P**uerto **R**ico.

Then he signed with the **B**rooklyn **D**odgers.

He played in two **W**orld **S**eries.

On **D**ecember 31, 1972, there was a tragic plane crash.

➤ **A.** Answer the questions using the example sentences.

1. Which capitalized word (or words) is the name of a person?
   Roberto Clemente Walker
   _____

2. Which capitalized word (or words) is a date?
   _____

3. Which capitalized word (or words) is a specific place?
   _____

4. Which capitalized words are a title that describes a specific team?
   _____

5. Which capitalized words are the name of a specific event?
   _____

➤ **B.** Edit the sentences. Rewrite each sentence by capitalizing proper nouns.

1. Have you ever been to puerto rico?
   _____

2. I would like to visit my cousin, pablo, there someday.
   _____

3. I have been told that it is nice there in december.
   _____

4. yoni said she would be happy to come with me.
   _____

VISIONS Unit 4 • Chapter 2 Roberto Clemente

VISIONS A Activity Book • Copyright © Heinle

Elements of Literature

Use with student text page 249.

Recognize Third-Person Point of View

Biographies are usually written in **third-person point of view.** This means that the author writes about the feelings and actions of other people, not his or her own feelings or actions.

➤ Rewrite the sentences in the third-person point of view. Replace the underlined words using the words *he, she, they, him, her, them, his, hers,* and *theirs.*

1. <u>I</u> was the youngest of four children.

   He (or she) was the youngest of four children.

2. <u>We</u> excelled in many sports.

   _____

3. <u>My</u> son joined the Pittsburgh Pirates in 1955.

   _____

4. Several times, the championship was <u>ours</u>.

   _____

5. The birth of <u>my</u> grandson made <u>me</u> very happy.

   _____

6. <u>Our</u> home in Puerto Rico is very important to <u>us</u>.

   _____

Word Study

Use with student text page 250.

Understand the Prefix un-

A **prefix** is a word part added to the beginning of a word. A prefix changes the meaning of a word. The prefix *un-* means "not."

un (not) + *fortunately* (happily) = *unfortunately* (not happily)

➤ **A.** Fill in the chart. Write the new words and their meanings. The first one has been done for you.

Word	New Word (*un-* + word)	Word	New Word (*un-* + word)
1. equal	*unequal*	**7.** fair	
2. happy		**8.** unimportant	
3. finished		**9.** familiar	
4. aware		**10.** knowing	
5. healthy		**11.** well	
6. usual		**12.** friendly	

➤ **B.** Complete the sentences using the words in the chart.

1. Our team kept losing to the Cubs. The two teams were ___*unequal*___.

2. He won't speak to anyone. I think he's _____.

3. Eating too much sugar will make you _____.

4. People can look very _____ when they frown.

5. Mrs. Thomas is always on time. It is very _____ for her to start her class late.

6. I didn't study. I was completely _____ that we had a Math test today.

Name _____ Date _____

Grammar Focus

Use with student text page 250.

Use Prepositional Phrases of Time

Prepositional phrases of time tell when something happened or will happen.

Roberto Clemente was born <u>on</u> *August 19, 1934.*

Use *at* and *in* to talk about clock time.

I'll be there.	at ten o'clock.
	at noon.
	at midnight.
	in an hour.
	in 15 minutes.

Use *on* and *in* to talk about calendar time.

Specific dates	It happened	on Monday, May 1. on May 1.
Days of the week		on Monday.
Months		in July.
Years		in 2004.

➤ **A.** Complete the sentences with *at, in,* or *on*.

1. I'll see you _____ Monday.

2. We usually have lunch _____ noon.

3. Can you meet me at the library _____ an hour?

4. My great-grandfather was born _____ 1900!

5. He was born _____ October 20.

6. The movie starts _____ 7:15.

7. School usually starts _____ August.

➤ **B.** Edit these sentences. Rewrite them and correct the errors in the prepositional phrases.

1. I have math class on 9:45 this morning. _____.

2. My family moved to this city on August. _____.

3. Independence Day is at July 4. _____.

4. Please call me in noon. _____.

5. Where were you living at 2000? _____.

6. I'll be 16 on a month. _____.

Name _____ Date _____

Grammar Focus

Use with student text page 250.

Learn More Prepositions of Time

Read this timeline of Marisol's day.

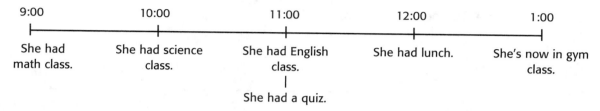

9:00	10:00	11:00	12:00	1:00
She had math class.	She had science class.	She had English class.	She had lunch.	She's now in gym class.
		She had a quiz.		

Math class was <u>before</u> science class.

English class was <u>after</u> science class.

Marisol had a quiz <u>during</u> English class.

She had only one class <u>since</u> lunch.

➤ **A.** Complete the sentences with *before, after, during,* or *since.* Use the timeline of Marisol's day.

1. Marisol had lunch _____ gym class.

2. She had lunch _____ English class.

3. She saw a movie about earthquakes. It was _____ science class.

4. She has had four classes and lunch _____ 9:00.

➤ **B.** Draw a timeline for your day. Then write sentences like the ones above.

Student
Handbook

Name _____ Date _____

From Reading to Writing

Use with student text page 251.

Edit a Biography

➤ Use the checklist to edit the biography you wrote in Chapter 2.

Editing Checklist for a Biography

Title of biography: _____

_____ **1.** I wrote the person's name and when and where he or she was born.

_____ **2.** I wrote down two or three important events in his or her life.

_____ **3.** I put the events in order.

_____ **4.** I used prepositional phrases to tell when things happened.

_____ **5.** I wrote in the third-person point of view, using pronouns such as *he, she, they,* or *it.*

_____ **6.** I used possessive nouns to tell what the person has or owns.

Across Content Areas

Use with student text page 251.

Use a Two-Column Chart to Take Notes

➤ Read the information. Take notes on the chart.

What is an earthquake?

Inside the Earth, things sometimes move around. When big pieces of rock break and move around, earthquakes can happen. We feel the ground shake. If you are inside a building during an earthquake, you will see things around you move.

The shaking of the ground is caused by **seismic waves.** Seismic waves are energy produced when the pieces of rock break and move.

How do we study earthquakes?

Scientists use computers and other tools to help them know how strong an earthquake is. Sometimes the scientists can **predict,** or guess, about when an earthquake might happen. These scientists are called **seismologists.**

Scientists have machines called **seismographs.** They show how strong an earthquake is. They give each earthquake a number on the **Richter Scale.** The higher the number is, the stronger the earthquake is.

Question	Answer
What is an earthquake?	
What is a seismic wave?	
What is a seismologist?	
What is the Richter Scale?	

VISIONS Unit 4 • Chapter 2 Roberto Clemente

Name _____ Date _____

Build Vocabulary

Use with student text page 253.

Find Antonyms

Antonyms are words that have opposite meanings. For example, *off* is the antonym for the word *on*.

➤ **A.** Write the letter of the antonym for each underlined word.

Word in a Sentence

1. ___c___ For Nelson Mandela, winning freedom was <u>paramount</u>.

2. _____ Mandela and others felt a strong <u>inclination</u> for equality.

3. _____ <u>Fortunately</u>, a lot of people agreed with Mandela.

4. _____ People all over the world like Mandela, and he is a <u>beloved</u> leader in his own country.

5. _____ He showed people that if you are <u>determined</u> enough to fight for your beliefs, you can change the world.

6. _____ A person who shows loyalty to his or her country is called a <u>patriot</u>.

Antonym

a. hated

b. unsure

c. unimportant

d. traitor

e. sadly

f. dislike

➤ **B.** Choose three of the antonyms and write a sentence of your own for each one.

1. _____

2. _____

3. _____

Writing: Punctuation

Use with student text page 262.

Use the Serial Comma

Use a **comma** to separate three or more items in a series.

I bought a *hat,* a *coat,* and a *pair of shoes* at the store.

Put a comma after each item before the word *and.*

➤ **A.** Read the groups of words. Add commas.

1. red, white, and blue

2. games puzzles and toys

3. coffee tea and hot chocolate

4. pencils pens and rulers

5. Toya Yvonne and Theresa

6. cookies pies and cakes

7. north northwest and northeast

8. Mr. Samuels Mrs. Anderson and Ms. Kitson

➤ **B.** Rewrite each sentence that needs serial commas. If the sentence does not need serial commas, write "OK."

1. Nelson Mandela is a patriot a leader and a great speaker.

   _____

2. He has brought hope to many people in his country.

   _____

3. He has won the respect of people in Africa Europe and America.

   _____

4. Others see him as a role model and a leader.

   _____

5. Presidents prime ministers and other leaders admire him.

   _____

6. In his speech, Mandela said, "The body the mind and the soul have been freed to fulfill themselves."

   _____

Name _____ Date _____

Elements of Literature

Use with student text page 263.

Write Dialogue

Dialogue is the exact words that characters say. Dialogue is shown by placing quotation marks ("...") around the words that are spoken. Remember these rules:
Quotation marks always appear in pairs.
Periods, commas, question marks, and exclamation marks go inside quotation marks.

Rolihahla's father said, "I am giving you this servant, Rolihahla."

➤ **A.** Underline the groups of words that show dialogue.

1. Nelson Mandela's father said, "I want my son to have an education."

2. The young Nelson said, "I will miss my father."

3. The tribal chief told Nelson, "I will raise you the way your father wished."

4. The chief said, "I understand that you wish to help your country."

5. The chief assured Nelson when he announced, "You will have an education."

6. Nelson promised, "I will help all people in my country become equal."

➤ **B.** Rewrite each sentence to include dialogue.

1. Nelson Mandela made speeches to say he cared about his country.

   Nelson Mandela said, "I care about my country."

2. Nelson Mandela made speeches to say that there is no easy road to freedom.

   Nelson Mandela said, "There _____."

3. Nelson Mandela made speeches to say none of us acting alone can achieve success.

   Nelson Mandela said, "None _____."

4. Nelson Mandela made speeches to say we must act together for the birth of a new world.

   Nelson Mandela said, "We _____."

5. Nelson Mandela made speeches to say let there be justice for all.

   Nelson Mandela said, "Let _____."

6. Nelson Mandela made speeches to say the body, the mind, and the soul have been freed to fulfill themselves.

   Nelson Mandela said, "The _____."

Word Study

Use with student text page 264.

Identify the Suffix *-ion*

When the suffix *-ion* is added to a word, it changes a verb into a noun.
The suffix *-ion* means "the act or state of being."

protect + *-ion* = protection

If the verb ends in *e*, you drop the *e* before you add *-ion*.

locate + *-ion* = location

➤ **A.** Form a noun by adding *-ion* to each verb. Write the new words in the chart.

Verb	Add *-ion*	New Word (Noun)
1. act	+ *-ion*	**1.** action
2. create		
3. predict		
4. migrate		
5. donate		
6. restrict		

➤ **B.** Change each verb to a noun ending in *-ion*. Then, write the word in the space. Remember, if a word ends in *e,* you drop the *e* before you add *-ion*.

1. (illustrate) A drawing is also called an _____.

2. (exhibit) The Air and Space Museum held an _____ to show the latest airplane designs.

3. (edit) The author wrote a second _____ of his book, because it was so popular.

4. (operate) The doctor was very good at doing a difficult _____.

5. (suggest) If you don't mind, I have a small _____ about your writing.

6. (pollute) We have to control air _____ so we can breathe clean air.

Grammar Focus

Use with student text page 264.

Recognize Commands with *Let*

A **declarative sentence** makes a statement. It ends with a period. A sentence that makes a request or gives an order is a **command** or an **imperative sentence.** A command shows strong feeling. It often ends with a period.

Imperative sentence (command): <u>Let</u> there be justice for all.

When Nelson Mandela used the word *let* in his speech, he was showing his strong feelings. The word *let* means "to allow."

Commands do not have subjects. The subject "you" is understood.

Let	Object or *There*	Simple Verb
Let	him	**show** us the way.
Let	there	**be** jobs for all.

➤ **A.** Change each statement to a command. Rewrite with the word *let.*

1. More people should get a good education.

   Let more people get a good education.

2. More children should grow up healthy.

   _____

3. Our water should be kept clean and pure.

   _____

4. Our nation should be strong.

   _____

5. Other nations should see us as a friend.

   _____

➤ **B.** Write a short speech about why you want to be president of the class. Use the word *let* in each sentence to show your strong feelings.

_____

_____

_____

_____

Grammar Focus

Understand Commands

To give a command to the person you are talking to, use the simple form of the verb.

Clean up your room.

Use a period or an exclamation point (**!**) to end a command. For a very strong command, use an exclamation point.

➤ Change each statement to a command. Punctuate each sentence with a period or an exclamation point.

1. You should write a note to your grandparents.

_____

2. You should thank them for the nice visit you had with them.

_____

3. You should tell them you enjoyed going camping.

_____

4. You should thank them for teaching you how to fish.

_____

5. You should tell them you've never been camping before.

_____

6. You should say you had a great time.

_____

Student
Handbook

From Reading to Writing

Use with student text page 265.

Write a Persuasive Speech

A **persuasive speech** is a speech in which you try to get the listener to agree with you.

➤ Write a speech to get people in your town to clean up litter. Answer the questions. Then write a paragraph based on the answers to the questions.

1. What is so bad about litter?

_____

_____

2. Why should other people worry about it?

_____

_____

3. Why should people listen to you?

_____

_____

4. What are some powerful words you can use to get people on your side?

_____

_____

5. What ideas do you have that will make a clean-up sound like a fun project?

_____

_____

Paragraph for a Persuasive Speech

_____

_____

_____

_____

_____

_____

_____

Across Content Areas

Use with student text page 265.

Make a Timeline

Make a timeline of part of your life.

➤ **A.** Choose three or four years that you want to tell about. Make notes below
on key events and dates. Use the events in the box for ideas.

> moved to _____
> first day at _____ school
> a special event with your family
> met a new friend
> learned a new skill

➤ **B.** Draw your timeline below. Include the important dates and events.

Dates: _____   _____   _____   _____   _____

|———————|———————|———————|———————|

Events: _____   _____   _____   _____   _____

Build Vocabulary

Use with student text page 267.

Understand Words in Context

Context is the words and sentences that surround a specific word.

Advertisements are made to *convince* you to buy something you do not need.

Convince means "to get someone to agree to do something."

➤ Match the underlined word to its definition. Use context clues to help you.

Word in a Sentence

1. _____ My grandfather has had a <u>lifelong</u> love for reading.

2. _____ It takes a lot of <u>patience</u> to learn to sew.

3. _____ The wind was so cold it felt <u>punishing</u> on my face.

4. _____ You work hard at your job, so you will be a good <u>provider</u> for your family someday.

5. _____ Gina told Roberto that she really wanted to be his friend, without any kind of <u>pretense</u>.

6. _____ Lena is so good in the kitchen that she will probably become a <u>chef</u>.

Definition

a. act that hides the real reason for doing something

b. cook

c. the ability to wait a long time

d. someone who earns money for his or her family

e. lasting through an entire life

f. causing pain

Name _____ Date _____

Writing: Spelling

Use with student text page 276.

Spell Regular Plurals

Add *-s* to change most singular nouns to the plural form. The **plural form** shows that there is more than one of something.

My father buys banana<u>s</u>.

➤ **A.** Rewrite the words in parentheses in their plural forms.

1. (pomegranate) We argue about the price of _____.

2. (scholar) I convince him it is the fruit of _____.

3. (orange) He's sure I'll be healthy so long as I eat more _____.

4. (seed) The orange has _____.

5. (tree) We too will come back like the orange _____.

6. (fact) He learned the simple _____ in life and lived by them.

➤ **B.** Rewrite the underlined singular noun in each sentence as a plural noun.

1. In summer, it's fun to go to the town <u>park</u>.

   _____

2. I am planning a picnic with my <u>friend</u>.

   _____

3. We'll make our favorite <u>snack</u>.

   _____

4. Then, we'll eat under the big <u>tree</u> in the park.

   _____

Elements of Literature

Use with student text page 277.

Recognize Imagery

Writers often use words that help readers create **images** (pictures) in their mind.

You will build beautiful houses where children sing and play.

The poet is writing about being an *architect*—a person who builds houses.
The poet also expresses how it might feel to live in the houses "where children sing and play."

➤ **A.** Draw a picture for each underlined image.

1. The orange has seeds and is perpetual
   (continuing forever).
   <u>We too will come back like the orange trees.</u>

3. <u>Colors spill over the ground from the
   rainbow overhead.</u>

➤ **B.** Write two or three words that would help a reader to get a better picture
   for each group of words. The first one has been done for you.

1. the sky on a sunny day
   a bright blue painting
   _____

2. a cloud
   _____

3. an orange
   _____

Name _____ Date _____

Word Study

Use with student text page 278.

Identify the Suffix *-er*

A **verb** is a word that shows action. If you add the suffix *-er* to some verbs, the verb changes into a noun. A **noun** is a word that names people, places, and things.

The suffix *-er* means "someone who does something."

paint + *-er* = painter (someone who paints)

➤ **A.** Complete the chart by adding *-er* to the verbs. If a verb ends in *e*, just

Word	Add *-er*	New Word	New Word Meaning
1. teach	+ *-er*	teacher	someone who teaches
2. sing			
3. write			
4. bake			
5. dance			
6. read			
7. own			
8. wash			

add *-r.* The first one has been done for you.

➤ **B.** Choose a word from the chart to complete each sentence.

1. Last year, our _____ showed us ways to remember how to spell difficult words.

2. I like reading books. I enjoy being a _____.

3. Every morning, the _____ puts 20 loaves of bread into a large oven.

4. You have a great voice. You should be a _____.

5. The windows are very clean. You are a great window _____.

6. The woman owns the land. She is called an _____.

7. She dances very well to the music. She is a great _____.

8. I like to write stories. I want to be a _____.

VISIONS A Activity Book • Copyright © Heinle

Name _____ Date _____

Grammar Focus

Use with student text page 278.

Recognize Reported Speech

Imagine that your friend Alma says this:

I like pomegranates.

There are two ways to write this: direct speech and indirect speech.

	Example	**Rules**
Direct Speech	Alma said, "I like pomegranates."	Use quotation marks. Give the exact words that someone said.
Reported Speech	Alma said that she likes pomegranates.	Do not use quotation marks. Uses dependent clause with *that*. Pronouns and verbs can change.

➤ **A.** Write *direct speech* or *reported speech.*

1. Tara said, "I always wanted to have a parrot."

_____

2. She said that she thinks they are beautiful birds.

_____

3. Tara said, "I think so."

_____

4. I told her that I had never seen so many colors.

_____

➤ **B.** Read these pairs of sentences. One uses direct speech, and the other uses reported speech. Complete the reported speech sentences.

1. My father says, "I will build a tree house."

My father says that _____ will build a tree house.

2. He tells me, "It is easy to do."

He tells me _____ it is easy to do.

3. My father says, "You and I will build it together."

My father says that _____ will build it together.

4. He says, "You will have a lot of fun in it."

_____ says that _____ will have a lot of fun in it.

149

Grammar Focus

Use with student text page 278.

Understand Complex Sentences

A **complex sentence** has two parts: an independent clause and a **dependent clause.**

An **independent clause** can stand alone. It is a complete sentence. For example:

> I learned a new dance.

A **dependent clause** is not a complete sentence. It cannot stand alone.

> that has many steps.

A dependent clause must be used with an independent clause.

> I learned a new dance that has many steps.

➤ **A.** Underline the independent clause in each sentence.

1. <u>I learned a new song</u> that has many words.

2. She learned to read music that has many notes.

3. He walked to a store that has many toys.

4. They like movies that have good actors.

5. We like sports that have good players.

6. She likes flowers that have many colors.

➤ **B.** Underline the dependent clause in each sentence.

1. I learned a new song <u>that has many words.</u>

2. She learned to read music that has many notes.

3. He walked to a store that has many CD's.

4. They like movies that have good actors.

5. We like sports that have good players.

6. She likes flowers that have many colors.

Student
Handbook

150

Name _____ Date _____

From Reading to Writing

Use with student text page 279.

Edit a Poem

➤ Use the checklist to edit the poem you wrote in Chapter 4.

Editing Checklist for a Poem

Title of poem: _____

_____ **1.** I used my web from Use Prior Knowledge.

_____ **2.** I wrote a poem with three stanzas.

_____ **3.** I used imagery to help my readers form pictures in their minds.

_____ **4.** I wrote a title that describes my role model.

_____ **5.** I used my best handwriting.

_____ **6.** I illustrated or decorated my poem.

Across Content Areas

Use with student text page 279.

Read Advertisements for Jobs

If you have ever looked in the "Classified" section of a newspaper, you know that there is a section called "Help Wanted." This is the section people read when they are looking for jobs.

Job advertisements are placed by *employers*—people who want to hire someone for a job.

Job advertisements use shortened forms of words called *abbreviations*. By using abbreviations, the advertisement

Abbreviations Used in Job Advertisements	
Word	**Abbreviation**
full time	f/t
part time	p/t
hour	hr
experience	exp
weekends	wknds

doesn't take up too much space. Here are some examples of abbreviations used in the "Help Wanted" section of the newspaper:

➤ **A.** Write an explanation for the following ad.

Baker's helper needed. F/t or p/t. $7.50/hr. No exp. necessary. Work wknds for summer. Call 555-342-1616 after 3 P.M.

_____

_____

_____

_____

➤ **B.** Write a job advertisement. Use the chart to help you with the abbreviations. Try to keep the advertisement as short as you can.

You are looking for a **dog walker** to work part time on the weekends. You will pay $6.00 an hour. You want a person who has experience with animals. If anyone is interested, they should call you at 555-661-4231.

_____

_____

_____

_____

Build Vocabulary

Use with student text page 289.

Study Word Meanings

Match Words and Definitions

➤ **A.** Match the underlined word in each sentence to its definition.

Anna wanted to <u>travel</u> from Houston to Mexico by airplane. She got a plane ticket and went to the airport. The <u>powerful</u> engines <u>propelled</u> the plane into the sky. The wings <u>tilted</u> to one side, turning the plane south. On the way to Mexico, the plane flew through clouds <u>floating</u> in the air. Anna kept her notebook with her so she could <u>record</u> her thoughts on paper. Anna used the journal to write about her <u>wonderful</u> trip.

Definitions

1. *record* _____ —copy events for review later on

2. _____ —leaned to one side

3. _____ —go from one place to another over a long distance

4. _____ —especially good

5. _____ —resting on top of a liquid or gas

6. _____ —very strong

7. _____ —pushed with force

➤ **B.** Complete the sentences. Use the vocabulary words from Exercise A.

1. I like to _____ by boat.

2. Last summer I went on a boat trip and had a _____ time!

3. I brought a journal so I could _____ my experiences on the trip.

4. The boat was very big and had a _____ engine that _____ us through the water.

5. A few times a large wave hit the boat and the boat _____.

6. Most of the time the boat _____ along calmly.

VISIONS Unit 5 · Chapter 1 Eye to Eye

Writing: Punctuation

Use with student text page 294.

Use Commas Between Adjectives

Commas (**,**) are used between two or more adjectives that describe the same noun.

The girl had **long, brown** hair.

Do not use a comma if the second adjective is part of a compound noun.

I go to a big **high school.**

High school is a compound noun made up of an adjective (*high*) and a noun (*school*). Therefore, there is no comma between *big* and *high*.

➤ **A.** Edit the sentences. Rewrite each sentence adding the missing comma.

1. The fox had a warm brown coat.

   _____

2. The girl asked the waitress for a shiny clean fork and a spoon.

   _____

3. The truck had big black heavy tires.

   _____

4. The dog watched the small quiet gray mouse.

   _____

➤ **B.** Edit this paragraph. Add commas where necessary. Mark out commas that are unnecessary.

It was a hot humid day. My friend and I decided to go to the big, public beach near our neighborhood. The tall white waves were waiting for us when we got there. I was wearing a red, bathing suit. My friend was wearing a yellow, bathing suit. The fluffy white clouds floated above us. The breeze was cool and gentle. We both had a long exciting day.

Elements of Literature

Use with student text page 295.

Identify Similes as Figurative Language

Figurative language helps readers form images or pictures in their minds. One type of figurative language is a simile. A **simile** uses the words *like* or *as* to compare one thing to another.

The dog ran **like** the wind.

The boy was **as** quiet as a mouse.

➤ **A.** Complete these similes. Use the phrases in the box.

    as hard as a rock
    as tall as a tree
    as fast as the wind
    as big as oranges
    as deep as an ocean
    as white as snow

1. The boy has eyes _as big as oranges_____.

2. My grandfather's hair was _____.

3. They gave us a piece of bread that was _____.

4. The train was _____.

5. The basketball player was _____.

6. He dived into a swimming pool that was _____.

➤ **B.** Match the first part of each simile with its ending.

1. Her hair looked like   **a.** thunder.

2. My dad's voice sounded like   **b.** a cat.

3. As the firefighter climbed the ladder, he   **c.** a mouse.
   moved like
                                                  d. a plate of spaghetti.
4. His room looked like
                                                  e. a tornado had hit it.
5. I didn't want the teacher to call on me.
   I sat there like

Name _____ Date _____

Word Study

Use with student text page 296.

Recognize Compound Adjectives

A **compound adjective** is an adjective formed from two other words. Many compound adjectives contain a **hyphen** (-). The meaning of a compound adjective can often be found by looking at the words it contains.

Compound Adjective	Meaning
slip-on shoes	shoes **that slip onto your feet**
built-in heater	a heater **that is built into something**
sixth-grade girl	a girl **who is in the sixth grade**

➤ **A.** Write the meaning of each compound adjective.

1. nice-looking hat   *a hat that looks nice* _____

2. far-reaching branches _____

3. over-done chicken   _____

4. twenty-foot bridge   _____

5. ready-made food   _____

6. well-oiled machine   _____

➤ **B.** Write a sentence for each compound adjective in Exercise A.

1. *Juan bought a nice-looking hat.* _____

2. _____

3. _____

4. _____

5. _____

6. _____

Grammar Focus

Use with student text page 296.

Use the Simple Past Tense

The **simple past tense** describes an action that began and ended in the past. **Regular past tense verbs** are formed by adding -*ed* to the end of the word.

She play**ed** her guitar.

Irregular past tense verbs are formed in different ways.

➤ **A.** Rewrite each sentence. Write the verb in past tense.

Some Regular and Irregular Verbs		
	Simple Form of Verb	**Past Form of Verb**
REGULAR VERBS	look	look**ed**
	tilt	tilt**ed**
	record	record**ed**
	vibrate	vibrat**ed**
	float	float**ed**
SOME IRREGULAR VERBS	give	**gave**
	see	**saw**
	feel	**felt**
	meet	**met**
	can	**could**

Present Tense Sentence

1. She likes to play basketball.

2. I join my friends after school.

3. They see the problem.

4. I feel the cold air.

5. They walk to school.

6. My grandparents give us nice presents.

Past Tense Sentence

1. *She liked to play basketball.*

2. _____

3. _____

4. _____

5. _____

6. _____

➤ **B.** Write three sentences about what you did yesterday. Use past tense verb forms.

1. _____

2. _____

3. _____

VISIONS **Unit 5 • Chapter 1** Eye to Eye

Name _____ Date _____

Grammar Focus

Use with student text page 296.

Use Past Tense Questions, Negatives, and Contractions

Use the auxiliary verb *did* to form questions and negative statements in the past tense.

Statements

Subject	Verb
The girls	worked. (past form)

Questions

Auxiliary	Subject	Verb
Did	the girls	work? (simple form)

Negative Statements

Subject	Auxiliary Verb + *Not*	Verb
The girls	did not didn't	work. (simple form)

The negative form *did not* can be contracted to *didn't*. Use contractions in speech and in informal writing.

➤ **A.** Write past tense questions using these subjects and verbs. The first one has been done for you.

1. *Did the boy dance?* _____

2. _____

3. _____

4. _____

5. _____

Subjects
the boy   the plant   your team Angela   the house
Verbs
grow   dance   laugh shake   win

➤ **B.** Write negative answers to the questions you wrote. Write the answers one time with *did not* and another time with *didn't*.

1. *The boy did not dance. The boy didn't dance.* _____

2. _____

3. _____

4. _____

5. _____

Student
Handbook

From Reading to Writing

Use with student text page 297.

Edit a Personal Narrative

➤ Use the checklist to edit the personal narrative you wrote in Chapter 1.

Editing Checklist for a Personal Narrative

Title of personal narrative: _____

What I did:

_____ **1.** I drew a picture of an unusual animal.

_____ **2.** I described where I was when I saw the animal and what it looked like.

_____ **3.** I used the pronouns *I, me, we,* and *us.*

_____ **4.** I used figurative language to compare the animal to something else.

_____ **5.** I used comparative and superlative adjectives to describe my animal.

_____ **6.** I used regular past tense verbs correctly.

_____ **7.** I used irregular past tense verbs correctly.

_____ **8.** I used negative past tense verbs and contractions correctly.

_____ **9.** I made needed corrections and rewrote my personal narrative.

Across Content Areas

Use with student text page 297.

Use Reference Sources

An **encyclopedia** is a book, web-site, or CD-ROM that gives information about many different topics. Read this encyclopedia entry. Then answer the questions.

This is the **title** of the entry.

The Humpback Whale

The **heading** tells what the section is about.

General Facts

Size and Color Humpback whales grow to be about 40 to 50 feet long. Humpback whales are black on the top of their body and white underneath. They have very long and narrow pectoral fins, which are the two fins on either side of their body.

The **subheading** tells what the paragraph is about.

Home Humpback whales live close to the coast in all of the world's oceans. Humpback whales travel between cold waters in the summer and warmer waters in the winter.

Diet Humpback whales eat small, shrimp-like sea animals and small fish. They also use their special teeth, or baleen, to strain very tiny sea animals out of the sea water.

346
Humpback Whale

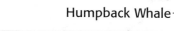 

Entry words make finding a title easier.

Photos and charts give more information.

Special Facts

Movement Humpback whales are one of the most skilled whales at propelling themselves out of the water. There are many photographs of humpback whales doing leaps and dives, like the one shown above.

Song Humpback whales make many sounds and talk to each other under water. Their sounds are called "songs" by scientists who study them. Groups of humpback whales that live in the same area of the ocean sing the same songs.

1. What is this encyclopedia entry about?

   _____

2. Write one heading in the entry.

   _____

3. Write two subheadings in the entry.

   _____

   _____

4. Circle the entry words on the page.

5. You want to learn how the humpback whale looks. What section in the entry would you read?

   _____

6. What other things would you like to know about the humpback whale? Write one question. Where could you go to find the answer?

   _____

   _____

Build Vocabulary

Use with student text page 299.

Explore Multiple Meaning Words

Sometimes words are spelled and pronounced the same but have different meanings. *Hard* can mean "firm" or "difficult."

Context clues are words that surround a word. They can help you understand the meaning of the unknown word.

Some Multiple Meaning Words	
Words	**Definition**
waste	a. garbage, unwanted leftovers b. a loss of something because it is not used well
right	a. the direction opposite of left b. correct, true
strange	a. not known before, unfamiliar b. odd, unusual
regular	a. normal, typical b. happening over and over, repeated

Choose the Definition

➤ Write the correct meaning of each word. Use context clues to help you.
   The first one has been done for you.

1. After she cut the paper, she put the <u>waste</u> in the garbage can.

   a. garbage, unwanted leftovers

2. I got the <u>right</u> answers on the test.

   _____

3. Elisa is wearing a <u>strange</u> hat.

   _____

4. The boys were <u>regular</u> visitors at the library because they went every day.

   _____

Writing: Spelling

Use with student text page 308.

Use *To, Too,* and *Two*

The words *to, too,* and *two* are all pronounced the same but have different meanings.

Word	Use	Example
To	A preposition The introduction to an infinitive	She went **to** church. He likes **to** write stories.
Too	An adverb meaning "also" An adverb meaning "more than enough"	I like to swim, and my friend does, **too.** Turn on the heat. It's **too** cold in here!
Two	A number	I have **two** sandwiches. Do you want one?

➤ **A.** Underline the correct word in each sentence.

1. Please give me (to/two) glasses of milk.

2. The girl went (too/to) the store with her mother.

3. He ate two pizzas. That's (too/two) much food for me.

4. When one boy laughed, the other boys laughed, (too/two).

5. How many times did he write the number (two/to)?

6. I like (to/too) ride my bike on Saturdays.

7. At school, we learn (to/too) read and (two/to) write.

8. Can I have a turn, (to/too)?

➤ **B.** Complete the paragraph with the word *to, too,* or *two.*

I like _____ go _____ school. I walk _____ school with _____ friends from my neighborhood. Their names are Lucia and Anabel. They like school, _____. Some boys and girls in my class live _____ far from school _____ walk. They ride on the bus.

➤ **C.** Write a sentence for each word.

1. two _____

2. to _____

3. too _____

Name _____ Date _____

Elements of Literature

Use with student text page 309.

Analyze Setting

Setting is the time and place of a story. The setting can be found by asking the questions *when?* and *where?*

Setting: *The Fun They Had*	
When?	**Where?**
The story takes place in the future in the year 2157.	The story takes place at Margie's house and in Margie's schoolroom.

➤ Read each story. Answer the questions.

1. It is night time. The moon is in the sky. A rattlesnake sits very still. It is waiting for its lunch. The desert is quiet.

   When does the story take place? _____

   Where does the story take place? _____

2. Miguel came home from school and went to his room. He could not wait to start the new book he got from the library. He turned on the light and got comfortable on his bed. He had an hour to read before it was time for dinner.

   When does the story take place? _____

   Where does the story take place? _____

3. The score is tied. The sun is setting. There are only three minutes left in the game. Alex runs for the ball and passes it to Marta. Marta stops the ball with her left foot and takes a shot at the goal. The crowd cheers as the ball goes past the goalie.

   When does the story take place? _____

   Where does the story take place? _____

Word Study

Use with student text page 310.

Use Latin Roots to Find Meaning

Root words are the words from which other words are made. Many words in English are based on root words from other languages, like Latin.

The English word *century* (100 years) is based on the Latin root word *centum,* which means "hundred."

Centum	
English Word	**Meaning**
century	one hundred years
centimeter	$\frac{1}{100}$ of a meter
centigrade	temperature measurement based on 100 degrees

➤ **A.** Complete the sentences. Use the words in the cluster map.

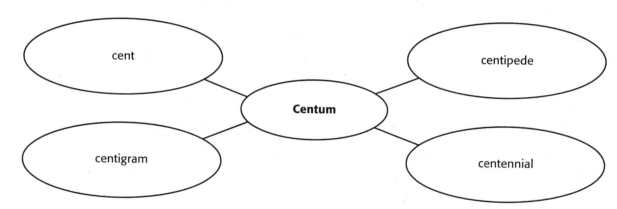

1. One hundred pennies make one dollar. Each penny is worth one _____.

2. The feather was very light. It weighed less than a _____.

3. The celebration of a 100 year anniversary is called a _____.

4. She saw the _____ and screamed. It had many legs and ran very fast.

➤ **B.** Match each English word to its Latin root word and definition.

English Words

1. regular _____

2. history _____

3. superior _____

4. fractions _____

Latin Roots

a. frangere: to break

b. historia: history

c. regula: rule

d. superus: being above

Grammar Focus

Use with student text page 310.

Use Dependent Clauses with *Because*

A **clause** is a group of words. It has a subject and a verb.

An **independent clause** (or main clause) is a complete sentence. It can stand alone.

A **dependent clause** is not a complete sentence. It cannot stand alone. It must be used with an independent clause. One kind of dependent clause starts with *because*. A *because* clause gives a reason. It answers the question *why?*

Independent Clause	Dependent Clause
Margie built the time machine	because she wanted to visit the past.

➤ **A.** Underline the dependent clause in each sentence.

1. They went to the beach <u>because it was hot.</u>

2. Anya wears red because it is her favorite color.

3. Sasha did not go to the movie because he was sick.

4. She went to sleep because it was bedtime.

5. He wore a winter coat because it was cold.

➤ **B.** Join the sentences using the word *because*. Write in complete sentences.

1. He got his hair cut. It was too long.

_____

2. The bird flew away. A cat walked by.

_____

3. Their team won the game. The fans were happy.

_____

4. She took a nap. She was tired.

_____

5. He was hot. He opened the window.

_____

VISIONS A Activity Book • Copyright © Heinle

Grammar Focus

Use with student text page 310.

Punctuate Complex Sentences

A **complex sentence** contains one independent clause and one or more dependent clauses.

Some Words That Signal a Dependent Clause	
Cause Words	**Time Words**
because since	after before when while

If a dependent clause beginning with cause words or time words comes first, put a comma (**,**) after it. If it comes after the independent clause, do not use a comma.

Because the store was busy**,** there was a line.

They arrived on time because they left early.

➤ **A.** Edit each sentence. Add a comma after the dependent clause.

1. Because the bread was old they bought crackers.

2. Irena went home when practice was over.

3. Because Helena was late she missed the play.

4. Before they went to bed they did their homework.

5. Anil read his book while his little sister was sleeping.

6. She wore a hat since it was raining.

➤ **B.** Write one sentence using a dependent clause with a cause word, and one with a time word.

1. _____

2. _____

Student
Handbook

From Reading to Writing

Use with student text page 311.

Revise, Edit, and Publish a Science Fiction Short Story

Use this worksheet to revise, edit, and publish the ending to the science fiction short story that you wrote in Chapter 2.

➤ **A. Revise** the draft of your story. Use the checklist to help with your revisions.

_____ **1.** The end of my story makes sense.

_____ **2.** I described the setting clearly.

_____ **3.** I described the characters clearly.

_____ **4.** I included a dependent clause with *because*.

➤ **B. Edit** your story. Use the checklist to help you make corrections.

_____ **1.** The first word of each sentence is capitalized.

_____ **2.** I checked the spelling of all unfamiliar words.

_____ **3.** I used periods, commas, and quotation marks correctly.

_____ **4.** The first line of each paragraph is indented.

➤ **C. Publish** your story. Prepare a final draft.

_____ **1.** Use clean, white paper.

_____ **2.** Write the story in your best handwriting or use a computer to type the story.

_____ **3.** Make sure to check for typing errors.

_____ **4.** Share your story ending with other people who have read "The Fun They Had."

Across Content Areas

Use with student text page 311.

Use a Chart to Compare

Online classes, audio classes, and **live classes** are three ways to learn.

In an **online class,** a student works on a computer. The computer program tells the student what to do and corrects the student's work. Students usually work alone. They may receive support through E-mail.	In an **audio class,** the student listens to an audiocassette or CD. Students usually work alone with little support. Audio classes to learn new languages are very common. Audio classes often come with a textbook.	In a **live class,** the student learns with a group of other students from a live person. The student receives assignments from the teacher and can have questions answered by the teacher. Students in live classes use textbooks or other books.

Each type of class has **advantages** and **disadvantages.**
An advantage is a positive thing or a benefit.
A disadvantage is negative thing or a drawback.

➤ **A.** Fill in the chart. Write advantages and disadvantages of each type of class.

	Advantages	Disadvantages
Online classes		
Audio classes		
Live classes		

➤ **B.** Answer the questions.

1. Which types of classes have you taken?

_____

2. Which type of class do you think is the best? Why?

_____

_____

Build Vocabulary

Use with student text page 313.

Use Synonyms and Antonyms

Synonyms are words that have similar meanings. **Antonyms** are words
that have opposite meanings. One way to understand new words is to find
words that mean the same or opposite.

Synonyms: fast/quick   hard/difficult

Antonyms: fast/slow   hard/easy

➤ **A.** Write *synonyms* or *antonyms* for each pair of words. Use your dictionary
to help you. The first one has been done for you.

1. fast/slow: *antonyms*

2. light/heavy: _____

3. nice/fine: _____

4. raw/cooked: _____

5. happy/joyful: _____

6. funny/serious: _____

➤ **B.** Find the word from the
box that matches the
synonym or antonym.
The first one has been
done for you.

Word	Definition
surprising	happening suddenly
quite	very
evidence	something that shows what is true, fact
pick	choose from several options
behavior	how a person acts
differently	not alike, not the same
patience	calmness, willingness to wait
give up	stop doing something

1. Synonym: actions

   He was responsible for his
   own *behavior* _____.

2. Synonym: proof

   Can you show
   _____ to
   support your ideas?

3. Synonym: completely

   He was _____ happy
   with his new job.

4. Synonym: select

   She had to _____ a
   dress to wear.

5. Antonym: anxiety

   _____ helps when
   learning new things.

6. Antonym: expected

   It was _____ that the
   cat liked the water.

7. Antonym: similarly

   One apple was shaped
   _____ than the others.

8. Antonym: continue

   The homework was difficult but he
   did not _____.

Writing: Capitalization

Use with student text page 322.

Capitalize and Punctuate Sentences

A **sentence** is a group of words that express a complete thought. The first word of a sentence is always capitalized.

He went for a walk.

The end of a sentence is always marked by a period (**.**), a question mark (**?**), or an exclamation point (**!**).

He went for a walk**.**

Did he go for a walk**?**

He walked on the most beautiful road**!**

The punctuation that is used at the end of a sentence depends on the meaning and expression of the sentence.

Punctuation	When It's Used
Period: **.**	used at the end of a statement or mild command
Question Mark: **?**	used at the end of a question
Exclamation Point: **!**	used at the end of a sentence that shows strong feelings

➤ Rewrite each sentence. Capitalize the words that begin sentences. Remember to use correct punctuation. The first one has been done for you.

1. how many apples do you have

   How many apples do you have?

2. she ran to the store

   _____

3. he behaves better after a nap

   _____

4. what a big dog

   _____

5. did you run out of patience with him

   _____

6. oh, no

   _____

7. my brother is good at puzzles

   _____

8. where is the evidence

   _____

Elements of Literature

Use with student text page 323.

Recognize Direct Address

Style is how authors use language to express themselves. **Direct address** is one element of style. This means that the author speaks directly to the reader using the pronouns *you* and *your.* Here is an example:

> **You** could probably think of some questions that the scientific method could help **you** answer.

➤ **A.** Underline the words that signal direct address.

Using Watercolors

There are several things you will need to get ready to paint with watercolors. First, pick the brushes that you want to use. Then select the paper. Your paper should be thick and able to hold a lot of water. You will need a clean, flat surface to work on and plenty of water. Choose the water jar that you like best. Open your paint set and you are ready to begin!

➤ **B.** Write a paragraph telling someone how to do something. Use the direct address style using the pronouns *you* and *your.*

_____

_____

_____

_____

_____

_____

_____

_____

_____

_____

_____

_____

_____

Name _____ Date _____

Word Study

Use with student text page 324.

Use Greek Word Origins to Find Meanings

Knowing the origins of words can help you understand their meanings. Many English words have Greek origins. The English word *philosophy* means "the study of truth." In Greek, *philosophia* means "love of wisdom."

Greek origin: *philos* "loving" + *sophos* "wise"

➤ **A.** Fill in the chart. Write the letter of the correct definition for each word.

Greek Origin	Greek Meaning	English Word	English Meaning
kata strephein	down to turn	catastrophe	1. *b*
dynamis	powerful	dynamic	2.
graphikos	write	graphic	3.
ethnos	nation	ethnic	4.
thermē statēs	heat that stands	thermostat	5.

English Definitions

a. having to do with racial or cultural groups and their customs

b. a sudden disaster, such as a flood or a fire

c. a device used to control temperature

d. active energy or force in motion

e. using pictures, diagrams, and drawing

➤ **B.** Complete each sentence using the words from the chart. The first one has been done for you.

1. The room was too hot, so I checked the ___*thermostat*___.

2. He is a _____ dancer. He has a lot of energy.

3. She likes to try _____ foods from different countries.

4. When the tornado hit the town, it was a _____.

5. Samir put a _____ of a tree in his report.

Grammar Focus

Use with student text page 324.

Use *Might* to Show Possibility

When the modal verb *might* is used in a sentence, it means "it is possible." To show that it is possible that an action may occur, use *might* with the simple verb form.

Subject + might + simple verb

They + might + play

They might play chess later.

➤ **A.** Reorder the words to create a sentence that shows possibility. The first one has been done for you.

1. visit museum the week. next might We

   We might visit the museum next week.

2. tire. might His new need bike a

   _____

3. canceled The might game be because rain. of

   _____

4. hypothesis correct. Her be might

   _____

5. try new He method. might a

   _____

6. win Carmen prize. spelling the might

   _____

➤ **B.** Write sentences that tell about your next birthday. Use *might* in each sentence.

1. _____

2. _____

3. _____

Name _____ Date _____

Grammar Focus

Use with student text page 324.

Use the Negative Form of *Might*

To show the negative form of *might,* the word *not* is placed between *might* and the verb in a sentence.

Subject + might not + verb

They   + might not + play chess later.

In this meaning, there is no contraction of *might not.*

➤ **A.** Rewrite these sentences using the negative form of *might.*

1. He might have a late dinner.

_____

2. The birds might fly south early this year.

_____

3. The music might be live.

_____

4. The city might build a new stadium.

_____

➤ **B.** Write sentences using *might not.* Choose one subject, one verb, and one phrase from the chart for each sentence. The first one has been done for you.

Subjects		Verbs	Phrases
The letter		take	an extra player.
She		be delivered	on time.
We	might not	have	tomorrow.
They		arrive	to the dance.
The plane		go	the train.

1. *The letter might not be delivered tomorrow.* _____

2. _____

3. _____

4. _____

5. _____

Student
Handbook

From Reading to Writing

Write a Business Letter

Use with student text page 325.

To apply for a job, people often write a letter to the company where they want to work. The letter tells about the person's experience, and why he or she wants the job.

➤ Write a letter to send with a job application. Use the form in the diagram.

(Street)
(City, State/Country, Zip Code)
(Date)

(Name)
(Street)
(CIty, State/Country, Zip Code)

Dear _____

_____
(State job you are interested in.)

_____
(Summarize why you are interested in the job.)

_____

First, _____
(Reason 1: Give details that tell what you could do for the company.)

_____

_____

Secondly, _____
(Reason 2: Give details that tell another thing you could do for the company.)

_____

_____

In conclusion, _____
(Restate your interest in the job.)

_____

Sincerely,

(Signature) _____

(Typed or printed name) _____

Across Content Areas

Use with student text page 325.

Find Information from a Bar Graph

A **graph** is a picture that shows data or groups of information. Graphs usually relate to numbers or amounts of things. A graph makes the relationship between different numbers easier to understand.

A **bar graph** uses bars to show numbers or amounts. The title of the graph is at the top. The bottom and sides of the graph have labels. The labels describe the information in the graph.

Sleep Habits for 1 Week

Understand Parts of a Graph

➤ **A.** Answer the questions. Use the graph.

1. What is the title of the graph? _____

2. What are the two labels that explain the graph?

   _____ _____

3. How many people's sleep habits are shown in the graph? _____

4. What do the numbers on the left side of the graph represent? _____

5. How many days does the graph show? _____

6. Which color shows Sue's sleep habits? _____

Analyze Information

➤ **B.** What can you learn about Sue, Piqui, and Ella's sleep habits from the graph?

1. How many hours did Piqui sleep on Tuesday? _____

2. How many hours did Ella sleep on Monday? _____

3. Who slept the most at the end of the week? _____

Build Vocabulary

Use with student text page 327.

Learn New Words in Context

➤ Write the underlined words in the paragraph next to their definition. Use context clues to help you. The first one has been done for you.

   The other night I dreamt that I was walking on Mars. <u>Particles</u> of dust were rising from the <u>reddish</u> <u>surface</u> as I walked. I saw many beautiful rocks and began to <u>collect</u> them along the way. At first I was walking across a <u>plain</u>. Then I saw a <u>crater</u> that was deep and <u>vast</u>. I threw a rock and listened. After a few seconds it <u>landed</u> on the <u>bottom</u> with a far away sound. When I woke up I realized it had been a dream. Even so, I felt like I had seen Mars <u>in person</u>.

Definition

1. _*bottom*_ the lowest part

2. _____ pick and gather into one place

3. _____ as if I were there

4. _____ the outside of something

5. _____ wide area of flat land

6. _____ came to rest on the ground

7. _____ somewhat red

8. _____ very small pieces of something

9. _____ a bowl shaped hole on the surface of a planet

10. _____ immense

Writing: Spelling

Use with student text page 340.

Use *Its* and *It's*

The words *its* and *it's* are pronounced the same, but they have different meanings. *Its* is the possessive form of the pronoun *it*.

Word	Meaning	Example
It's	Contraction of *it is*	**It's** my turn.
Its	Possessive form of *it*	I like everything about my school except **its** library—it's too small.

➤ **A.** Complete each sentence using the correct form, *its* or *it's*.

1. When they bought the house, _____ walls were falling down.

2. The newspaper says _____ going to be sunny today.

3. The moon gets _____ glow from the sun.

4. I wonder what _____ like on other planets.

5. Do you know if _____ hot on Venus?

6. The cat likes to take _____ nap on the green blanket.

7. A plant needs _____ roots to absorb water.

8. At twelve o'clock midnight _____ going to be a new day!

➤ **B.** Write *its* or *it's* to replace each underlined phrase. The first one has been done for you.

1. The town's library was very large. *Its* _____

2. Do you know if the game is going to start soon? _____

3. The rock's surface was red. _____

4. The planet's orbit took 365 days. _____

5. I think the clock is slow. _____

6. The store is two miles from my house. _____

7. They reported that the probe's travels were successful. _____

Elements of Literature

Use with student text page 341.

Explore Graphic Aids

A **graphic aid** is a picture that supports the information in a text. Graphic aids include charts, diagrams, photographs, and illustrations. They help readers understand information.

➤ Answer the questions using the information in the graphic aid.

Planet	Order from Sun	Average Temperature	Size	Water	Time to Rotate
Mercury	1	−183°C night 407°C day	a little larger than Earth's moon	None	59 Earth days
Venus	2	450°C	about the same size as Earth	None	Longer than 1 Venus year
Mars	4	−125°C winter 0°C summer	about ½ the size of Earth	Traces of water vapor	24 hours

1. What would be the fastest way to find the size of each planet: read a text or look at the chart?

   _____

2. What might a text tell the reader that a chart cannot?

   _____

   _____

3. Why do you think it's helpful to use a text together with graphic aids?

   _____

   _____

   _____

4. How many days does it take Mercury to rotate?

   _____

   _____

5. What is the average temperature of Venus?

   _____

6. How big is Mars compared to Earth?

   _____

   _____

7. Does Mars have water?

   _____

8. Is Venus or Mercury closer to the sun?

   _____

Word Study

Use with student text page 342.

Recognize Words and Sounds with the Spelling *oo*

There are two ways to pronounce *oo* in English. The two sounds can be heard in the words *moon* and *good*. There are no rules for when to use each pronunciation. You must learn which way to pronounce *oo* when you learn each word.

Dictionaries have special symbols they use to show the pronunciations of words. The symbol for the *oo* sound in *moon* is ü. The symbol for the sound in *good* is u̇.

Word	Pronunciation
moon	(mün)
good	(gu̇d)

Practice with *oo*

➤ **A.** Ask someone to pronounce these words for you, or find the pronunciations in a dictionary. Write ü or u̇ for each word.

1. too __ü_____   5. cool _____

2. shook _____   6. look _____

3. pool _____   7. cook _____

4. school _____   8. book _____

➤ **B.** Write the *oo* words you found in the dictionary into the chart.

Words Pronounced like *moon* (mün)	Words Pronounced like *good* (gu̇d)

Grammar Focus

Use with student text page 342.

Identify Superlative Adjectives

Superlative adjectives are adjectives that compare more than two nouns. Superlative adjectives often end in *-est*. Superlative adjectives show that the noun being described is "super," "above," or "the most" in comparison with the others.

Sofia wrote a **long** report.

Sofia wrote the **longest** report in the class.

➤ Complete each group of sentences using the correct adjective form from the chart. Some adjectives can be used with more than one sentence.

Adjective	Superlative
light	lightest
smart	smartest
nice	nicest
calm	calmest
fresh	freshest
near	nearest

1. **a.** She chose the ___lightest___ of all the colors for her painting.

   b. She chose ___light___ colors for her painting.

2. **a.** She was the _____ student in the class.

   b. She was a _____ student.

3. **a.** That store sells _____ fruit.

   b. That store sells the _____ fruit anywhere!

4. **a.** He said it was a _____ day.

   b. He said it was the _____ day of the year.

5. **a.** The man sitting in the back was the _____ person.

   b. The people on the train were _____ and quiet.

6. **a.** Of the three, Ernesto was the _____ to the door.

   b. Tom, Ernesto, and Julio were _____ the door.

Grammar Focus

Use with student text page 342.

Use Superlative Adjectives

Using superlative adjectives makes writing more precise or accurate.

He has a **short** name.

He has **the shortest** name of anyone in his town.

The reader gets more specific information from the word *shortest* than from the word *short*. Use *the* before most superlative adjectives.

➤ **A.** Fill in the chart. Write the superlative form of each adjective by adding *-est* at the end. When the word ends in *e*, add *-st*.

➤ **B.** Rewrite each sentence using the superlative form of the underlined adjective. Then choose a completion to the sentence.

Adjective	Superlative
bright	the
soft	the
large	the
quiet	the
close	the
neat	the
fast	the

1. The sun is <u>bright</u>.

   _____

2. The song was <u>soft</u>.

   _____

3. The class was <u>large</u>.

   _____

4. The street was <u>quiet</u>.

   _____

5. The planet is <u>close</u>.

   _____

6. Her desk was <u>neat</u>.

   _____

7. The horse was <u>fast</u>.

   _____

in the concert

to the sun

in the class

in the race

thing in the sky

in the school

in the neighborhood

Student
Handbook

From Reading to Writing

Use with student text page 343.

Write a Fictional Description

What if there were another planet in the solar system? Where would it be? What would it look like? What would the temperature, atmosphere, and rotation time be on that planet?

➤ Write a description of a fictional planet in the solar system. Use what you already know about the Sun and the planets to help you.

1. **Brainstorm:** Use the chart to help you outline the details about your fictional planet.

Name of Planet _____	Details
Order from Sun	
Type of Atmosphere	
Water?	
Temperature	
Life forms?	
Size	
Time to Rotate	

2. **Write a draft:** Use the chart to write a draft of your description. Use superlative adjectives in your writing.

3. **Revise your draft:** Use this checklist to help you revise.

_____ My introduction is clear and easy to understand.

_____ The main point in each paragraph is clear.

_____ Each point is described in detail.

_____ My conclusion is interesting and summarizes my writing.

4. **Edit and proofread:** Proofread your writing for spelling, capitalization, and punctuation errors.

5. **Publish:** Rewrite your fictional description in your best handwriting.

Across Content Areas

Use with student text page 343.

Compare Graphic Aids

Information can be presented visually in many different ways. Graphs, charts, diagrams, drawings, and photographs are just a few examples.

➤ **A.** Look at the two examples of graphic aids. Write how each one might help the reader better understand the text.

Planet	Order from Sun	Size
Mercury	1	about the size of Earth's moon
Venus	2	same size as Earth
Earth	3	about $\frac{1}{100}$ size of the Sun
Mars	4	half the size of Earth

1. This graphic aid can help the reader understand the text because _____

_____

_____.

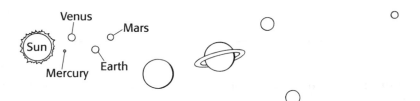

2. This graphic aid can help the reader understand the text because _____

_____

_____.

➤ **B.** Explain which graphic aid is more helpful to you.

_____

_____

VISIONS Unit 5 • Chapter 4 The Solar System

VISIONS A Activity Book • Copyright © Heinle

Build Vocabulary

Use with student text page 353.

Identify and Use Synonyms

Many words in English have synonyms—words with similar meanings. You can often replace words with other words in a sentence.

My teacher asked me a <u>simple</u> question.

My teacher asked me an <u>easy</u> question.

Word and Definition

draped covered   **incline** a hill

drop fall   **smoothed** pressed out

distant faraway   **giggled** laughed

handful small amount   **silent** makes no sound

➤ Underline each word or group of words with similar meanings to the words in the box. Rewrite each sentence using the new words.

1. She <u>laughed</u> when she sat down on the ground.

   She giggled when she sat down on the ground.
   _____

2. The girl and her papa were quiet.

   _____

3. The girl and her papa walked up the hill.

   _____

4. They looked out over fields covered with vines.

   _____

5. The grapes were ripe and ready to fall off the vines.

   _____

6. The girl heard the faraway sound of birds.

   _____

7. Her papa gave the girl a small amount of grapes.

   _____

8. She pressed out the wrinkles in her dress.

   _____

Writing: Punctuation

Use with student text page 358.

Use Capitalization and Punctuation with Dialogue

Use Capitalization with Dialogue

Dialogue is the exact words that characters say. Dialogue is shown by placing quotation marks (" ") around the words that are spoken.

Dialogue uses capitalization in a special way. Begin a sentence of dialogue with a capital letter.

"**T**his whole valley breathes and lives," he said.

Papa said, "**Y**ou can only feel the earth's heartbeat when you are quiet."

A. ➤ Underline the word in each sentence that should be capitalized. The first one has been done for you.

1. "<u>our</u> land is alive," Papa said.

2. Then he said, "it gives us the grapes."

3. Papa asked, "did you know you can feel the land breathe?"

4. After a moment, she asked, "why can't I feel it?"

5. "you must be patient, Esperanza," Papa said.

Use Punctuation with Dialogue

Use a **comma** to separate dialogue from the person who said it. Commas may come before the dialogue or after it. Sometimes a comma replaces a period at the end of dialogue.

"This whole valley breathes and lives**,**" he said.

Papa said**,** "You can only feel the earth's heartbeat when you are quiet."

B. ➤ Edit these sentences. Rewrite each sentence by correcting the errors in the use of commas.

1. "The mountains welcome us" Papa said.

_____

2. Papa said. "You can feel the earth's heartbeat."

_____

3. Esperanza giggled and said "I want to feel it."

_____

Elements of Literature

Use with student text page 359.

Analyze Characters

The people in a story are the **characters**. Esperanza and Papa are characters in the story "Esperanza Rising." The chart shows some things we can learn about characters when we analyze them.

Ways to Analyze Characters	
Relationships	How do characters feel about other characters?
Changes	How do characters change?
Traits	What do characters look like? How do they act?
Motivation	Why do characters do something?
Conflict	What problems do characters have?
Point of View	What are the characters' opinions?

➤ Read this paragraph from "Esperanza Rising." As you read, ask yourself: What did I learn about the characters from this paragraph?

"Our land is alive, Esperanza," said Papa, taking her small hand as they walked through the gentle slopes of the vineyard. Leafy green vines draped the arbors and the grapes were ready to drop. Esperanza was six years old and loved to walk with her papa through the winding rows, gazing up at him and watching his eyes dance with love for the land.

➤ Circle the correct answers. Use the paragraph to help you.

1. How did Esperanza feel about her father?
   a. She loved her father.
   b. She walked in the vineyard.

2. What was Papa's opinion of the land?
   a. He thought it was good for growing grapes.
   b. He thought it was very important and special and and he loved it.

3. Why did Esperanza like to walk with her papa in the vineyard?
   a. She liked to see how much he cared for the land.
   b. She liked to see the grapes and the arbors.

Word Study

Use with student text page 360.

Distinguish Denotative and Connotative Meanings

The **denotative meaning** of a word is the literal (exact) meaning of a word. For example, the denotative meaning of *alive* is "living, functioning."

You must eat to stay <u>alive</u>.

A **connotative meaning** has to do with the images and feelings we connect to a word. The connotative meaning of *alive* is "full of energy."

The park was <u>alive</u> with activities and music.

The chart shows the denotative and connotative meanings of some words.

Word	Denotative Meaning	Connotative Meaning
swallowed	took in food into the throat from the mouth	held back from expressing
distant	far away	not friendly; cold
heart	an organ that pumps blood through the body	the most important or central part of something
asleep	sleeping	not paying attention

A. ➤ Read the sentences and look at the underlined words. Write *denotative* or *connotative*.

denotative _____   **1.** The heart beats faster after a person exercises.

_____   **2.** Pedro swallowed his words and decided not to speak.

_____   **3.** The goalie was asleep when the other team scored.

_____   **4.** I never see Angelina. Her family moved to a distant city.

_____   **5.** The capitol building is in the heart of the city.

_____   **6.** Grandfather was asleep on the couch.

_____   **7.** I think Mauro is mad at me. He is acting very distant.

_____   **8.** Rosa swallowed a large piece of the apple.

B. ➤ Write two sentences using one of the words in the chart. In one sentence, use the denotative meaning. In the other sentence, use the connotative meaning.

1. _____

2. _____

Grammar Focus

Use with student text page 360.

Identify Possessive Adjectives

A **possessive adjective** is a word that describes a noun. It tells who or what owns something. Look at these examples. The possessive adjectives are boldfaced:

José's jacket is on the chair. **His** gloves are in **its** pocket.

Subject Pronouns	Possessive Adjectives	Examples
I	my	That's **my** backpack.
you	your	Where's **your** homework?
she	her	I like **her** hair.
he	his	**His** dad works in a bank.
it	its	We like our house, but **its** kitchen is small.
we	our	**Our** school has a great basketball team.
they	their	The students turned in **their** reports.

A. ➤ Match each phrase in Column A to a phrase in Column B to make a sentence. The first one has been done for you.

1. __*d*__ Esperanza liked to walk with   **a.** its fruit.

2. _____ Papa and Esperanza joined   **b.** his land.

3. _____ Papa was proud of   **c.** her cheeks.

4. _____ They lay down on   **d.** her papa.

5. _____ Each vine was ready to drop   **e.** their stomachs.

6. _____ The sun warmed   **f.** their hands.

Name _____ Date _____

Grammar Focus

Use with student text page 360.

Use Possessive Adjectives

Remember that a possessive adjective must agree with the person or thing that is the owner.

Incorrect: The girl brought <u>his</u> lunch to school.

Correct: The girl brought <u>her</u> lunch to school.

Incorrect: The students rode <u>her</u> own bicycles.

Correct: The students rode <u>their</u> own bicycles.

Incorrect: The tree dropped <u>their</u> leaves.

Correct: The tree dropped <u>its</u> leaves.

Notice the possessive adjective *its* in the example above. Be careful to spell it correctly. Do not confuse *its* with *it's*. *It's* is a contraction for *it is*.

A. ➤ Complete each sentence with the correct possessive adjective. Use the chart on page 189 to help you.

1. Esperanza smoothed _____ dress.

2. Papa put a handful of earth in _____ hand.

3. "_____ land is smiling at us," Papa said.

4. Esperanza and her father put _____ ears to the ground.

5. "Wait, Esperanza, and the fruit will fall into _____ hand," Papa told her.

6. The vineyard was ready to drop all of _____ grapes.

7. Esperanza's father cared a lot about _____ vineyard.

8. Papa said that when you lie down on the land, you can feel _____ heart beating.

B. ➤ Write four sentences using possessive adjectives. Use a different possessive adjective in each sentence.

1. _____

2. _____

3. _____

4. _____

Student
Handbook

Name _____ Date _____

From Reading to Writing

Use with student text page 361.

Edit a Fiction Story

➤ Use the checklist to edit the fiction story you wrote in Chapter 1.

Editing Checklist for a Fiction Story

Title of story: _____

What I did:

_____ 1. I wrote about how a character changes as events happen.

_____ 2. I made up a character.

_____ 3. I decided on a setting for my story.

_____ 4. I organized my story in three paragraphs.

_____ 5. I wrote the beginning of my story in the first paragraph.

_____ 6. I wrote the middle of my story in the second paragraph.

_____ 7. I wrote the end of my story in the third paragraph.

_____ 8. I indented my paragraphs.

_____ 9. I used past tense verbs to show events that already happened.

Across Content Areas

Use with student text page 361.

Use Outlining to Take Notes

➤ Read this article about grapes. Use an outline to take notes about the article. An outline helps you organize the information you read. Write your outline in the space provided.

GRAPE GROWING

History

People have been growing grapes in vineyards for thousands of years. Grape seeds have been found in very old tombs in Egypt. Many years ago, people in the Middle East grew grapes. Over time, grape growing spread to Europe, Africa, South America, and North America.

Where Grapes Grow

Grapes grow best in certain types of climates. California has a good climate for growing grapes. It has mild winters and a long, dry growing season. The soil also affects how well grapes grow. Grapes thrive in soil that drains water well.

How Grapes Are Used

Grapes can be used in many ways. Some growers produce fresh table grapes. When the fruit is mature, it can be eaten fresh. Other growers dry the grapes. Raisins are dried grapes. Many growers crush their grapes. When the grapes are crushed, the juice is pressed out. It is collected and made into grape juice.

Outline

Topic _____

A. (First Heading) _____

    1. (Detail) _____

    2. (Detail) _____

    3. (Detail) _____

B. (Second Heading) _____

    1. (Detail) _____

    2. (Detail) _____

    3. (Detail) _____

C. (Third Heading) _____

    1. (Detail) _____

Build Vocabulary

Use with student text page 363.

Identify New Words in Context

Context is the words and sentences that surround a specific word.

I held out my hand and she placed the money in my palm.

Palm means "the inside part of the hand."

A. ➤ Match each underlined word to its definition. Use the context clues for help.

Years ago, companies gave away picture cards along with their products. The cards
showed baseball players. The value of some old baseball cards has increased. Only a few
of them still exist. These rare cards may be worth hundreds of dollars. Some people
know instantly what a card is worth. They can tell if it is in good condition and if it is
old. In old cards, players look stiff, their heads swiveled right or left. Their hair is
usually parted in the middle.

Word in a Sentence	Definitions
1. _____ products	**a.** immediately, without delay
2. _____ value	**b.** how much something is worth
3. _____ exist	**c.** the things a company sells
4. _____ rare	**d.** turned
5. _____ instantly	**e.** one of a very few, unusual
6. _____ condition	**f.** combed to leave a dividing line
7. _____ swiveled	**g.** remain
8. _____ parted	**h.** how something is; for example, how something looks

B. ➤ Complete each sentence with a vocabulary word. Use context clues to help you.

1. A few old baseball uniforms still _____.

2. Many old photos show people with their hair _____ in the middle.

3. Today, companies use the names of baseball players on many of their
_____.

4. If you wash a baseball shirt carefully, it will stay in good _____.

Writing: Capitalization

Use with student text page 374.

Capitalize Proper Nouns and Punctuate Sentence Endings

Capitalize Proper Nouns

Proper nouns name specific people, places, and things. Proper nouns are always capitalized.

Noun   Proper Noun

The baseball team plays in a city. The baseball team plays in Pittsburgh.

A. ➤ Underline the word or words in each sentence that should be capitalized. Rewrite the sentence correctly. The first one has been done for you.

1. In the united states, early baseball cards were printed by companies.

In the United States, early baseball cards were printed by companies.

2. Miss young asked joe stoshack to clean out her attic.

_____

3. The star baseball player of the pittsburgh pirates was honus wagner.

_____

4. Later, joe rode his bike past sheppard park and founders square.

_____

5. Honus wagner asked the american companies to withdraw his card.

_____

Punctuate Sentence Endings

Punctuation at the end of a sentence tells that the sentence has come to a full stop. Use a period (.) at the end of a statement. Use a question mark (?) at the end of a question. Use an exclamation point (!) at the end of an exclamation (words in a sentence that show strong feeling).

B. ➤ Add the correct punctuation mark to the end of each sentence.

1. The baseball card was in perfect condition _____

2. How much is the card worth _____

3. Joe wondered why no one had found it before now _____

4. Good play _____

5. The card belonged to Miss Young _____

Elements of Literature

Use with student text page 375.

Recognize Style, Tone, and Mood

Authors use **style, tone,** and **mood** to express themselves.

	Style, Tone, and Mood	
Element	**Definition**	**Ask Yourself:**
Style	How an author uses language	Did the author use: Long or short words? Long or short sentences? Figurative language? Formal or informal language? Humorous or serious language?
Tone	The author's own attitude about the subject	Is the author's attitude: Positive? Negative? Approving? Disapproving?
Mood	The feeling the author wants you to get	Does the reader feel: Suspense? Excitement? Fear? Sadness?

A. ➤ Read the paragraph from *Honus and Me.* Joe is talking to himself. Think about the paragraph's style, tone, and mood.

Almost as quickly, my brain came up with reasons I shouldn't feel badly. Miss Young herself said that money wouldn't do her any good, so why *shouldn't* I keep the card? After all, *she* told me to throw the stuff away. If I hadn't found the card, *she* wouldn't have found it. It would have ended up buried in a landfill someplace, worth nothing to anyone. Finder's keepers, right?

➤ Read each sentence. Write *style, tone,* or *mood.*

1. The author uses words that a boy would say to himself.

_____

2. The author seems to disagree with Joe's reasons for keeping the card.

_____

3. Readers feel unsure about what Joe will do.

_____

4. The sentences almost run together to make it seem as if they are inside Joe's head.

_____

Word Study

Use with student text page 376.

Use a Thesaurus or Synonym Finder

A **thesaurus** and a **synonym finder** are books that list synonyms. **Synonyms** are words that have similar meanings.

A thesaurus and a synonym finder are not only in book form. Many computers come with a thesaurus on them. You can also find a thesaurus or a synonym finder on the Internet.

Here are some examples of entries in a synonym finder.

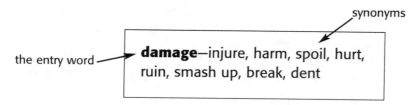

synonyms

the entry word ⟶ **damage**—injure, harm, spoil, hurt, ruin, smash up, break, dent

border edge, margin, rim, frame, boundary
dashed rushed, hurried, raced, ran, left quickly
hauled towed, dragged, pulled, lugged, heaved
junk useless items, rubbish, scrap, garbage, trash, litter
picture image, portrait, photograph, photo, print
solemn grave, serious, sad, glum, formal

➤ Rewrite each sentence with a synonym to replace the underlined word. Use the synonyms in the box. The first one has been done for you.

1. The Honus Wagner baseball card had a white <u>border</u>.
   The Honus Wagner baseball card had a white edge.
   _____

2. Miss Young asked Joe to clean the <u>junk</u> out of her attic.

   _____

3. Joe <u>hauled</u> the junk out to the curb.

   _____

4. Each card had a <u>picture</u> of a baseball player on it.

   _____

5. In his picture, Honus Wagner had a <u>solemn</u> look on his face.

   _____

6. As soon as he finished the job, Joe <u>dashed</u> away.

   _____

Grammar Focus

Use with student text page 376.

Understand and Use the Past Perfect Tense

The **past perfect tense** names an action that took place before another action or event in the past. The past perfect tense is formed by using *had* with the **past participle** of a verb.

Past participles are formed by adding *–d* or *–ed* to the simple verb. A sentence in the past perfect tense often has two verbs, one in the past tense and one in the past perfect tense. The past perfect tense shows that the action happened before something else.

Before he <u>left</u>, Joe <u>had received</u> some money from Miss Young.

Past Tense Verb	Past Perfect Tense Verb
Before Joe <u>found</u> the cards,	nobody <u>had</u> <u>touched</u> it for years.
Everyone <u>knew</u>	what <u>had</u> <u>happened</u> to him.
Before he <u>rode</u> his bike,	Joe <u>had</u> <u>cleaned</u> the attic.

A. ➤ Write the past tense verb and the past perfect tense verb in each sentence. The first one has been done for you.

1. Joe had collected baseball cards long before he found the Honus Wagner card.

   Past: *found* _____   **Past Perfect:** *had collected* _____

2. He thought he had discovered the most valuable baseball card in the world.

   Past: _____   **Past Perfect:** _____

3. Even though Miss Young had handed him ten dollars, Joe kept the card.

   Past: _____   **Past Perfect:** _____

B. ➤ Complete the sentences with the past perfect tense or the past tense. Use the verbs in parentheses. Remember, the past perfect tense shows something that happened before something else.

1. When I woke up, I smelled something delicious. My mother _____ (cook) my favorite breakfast!

2. When Alicia got to the bus stop, she realized that she _____ (miss) it.

3. We _____ (arrived) at the mall, and our friends were there.

4. I _____ (want) to eat the cookies, but my sister had taken them for her lunch.

5. Everyone applauded when the president _____ (enter) the room.

Grammar Focus

Use with student text page 376.

Use the Past Perfect Tense in Questions, Negatives, and Contractions

To form a **past perfect tense** question, put the auxiliary verb *had* in front of the subject.

<u>Had</u> Joe <u>noticed</u> the card before he finished the attic?

To form a negative, use *not* after *had*. The contracted form is *hadn't*.

Joe <u>had not returned</u> the card before he left.

The company <u>hadn't printed</u> many cards before Honus stopped them.

Past Perfect Tense	Negative (full form)	Negative (contraction)
had existed	had not existed	hadn't existed
had hauled	had not hauled	hadn't hauled
had stopped	had not stopped	hadn't stopped
had dashed	had not dashed	hadn't dashed

A. ➤ Write each sentence as a question. The first one has been done for you.

1. Miss Young had handed Joe money before he left.

   Had Miss Young handed Joe money before he left?

2. Joe had uncovered the card on the floor after he moved some junk.

   _____

3. A few cards had reached the public before Honus stopped the printing.

   _____

4. Joe had arrived at Miss Young's house after she asked him for help.

   _____

B. ➤ Write sentences using the full negative form and negative contractions.

1. _____

   _____

2. _____

   _____

Student
Handbook

From Reading to Writing

Use with student text page 377.

Write to Inform

When you write to **inform,** you present facts and explain ideas about something.

➤ Write a paragraph to inform readers about objects that you or someone you know collects.

Things People Collect

trading cards	stamps	colored glass bottles	model cars
action figures	dolls	old jewelry	

1. Write a topic sentence.

2. Write detail sentences.

3. Write a concluding sentence.

1. Write a topic sentence. State the main idea; tell what objects you are going to write about.

2. Write detail sentences. Give specific information about the objects: facts, examples, descriptions, or reasons.

3. Write a concluding sentence. End the paragraph: restate the main idea, give your opinion, or draw a conclusion.

Across Content Areas

Use with student text page 377.

Use Different Media

Forms of **media** include newspapers, photographs, television, encyclopedias, and Internet sites. You can choose forms of media to present your information in the best way.

Excerpt from an Encyclopedia Article

Honus Wagner. Real name: John Peter Wagner. Nicknames: Honus, Hans, the "Flying Dutchman." Born Feb. 24, 1874, Carnegie, PA. Died Dec. 6, 1955, Carnegie, PA. American professional baseball player. Some believe he was the finest all-around player in the history of the National League. Wagner played for the Louisville Colonels from 1897 through 1899. He played for the Pittsburgh Pirates from 1900 through 1917. He was a popular figure in Pittsburgh, and coached the Pirates from 1933 to 1951.

Quotations from an Internet site

WAGNER, PITTSBURG

"While Wagner was the greatest shortstop, I believe he could have been the number one player at any position he might have selected. That's why I vote him baseball's foremost all-time player." — John McGraw

➤ Answer the questions. Use the forms of media to help you.

1. From this part of the encyclopedia article, I learned

_____

2. From this photograph, I learned

_____

3. From these quotations from an Internet site, I learned

_____

Build Vocabulary

Use with student text page 379.

Use Words About Egypt

The author of *The Boy King* used the words below in her descriptions of Tutankhamen and the country he ruled.

Egypt a country in northeast Africa
Egyptian a person from Egypt
pharaoh a title of kings and queens in ancient Egypt
scholars people who have learned a lot about a subject
ancient very old
kingdom a country ruled by a king or queen
tomb a burial room or grave with a monument over it
chariot a horse-drawn, two-wheeled cart used in ancient times
throne the power or rank of a king; the chair a king sits on

➤ Choose a word to complete each sentence. Write it in the space.

1. Tutankhamen was an __Egyptian__ boy who became ruler.

2. He was trained from a young age because he was in line for the __egyet__.

3. According to present-day __Pharaoh__, Tutankhamen liked sports.

4. The ruler's palace in __scholars__ was painted in bright colors.

5. When he was about nine, Tutankhamen became the __ancient__.

6. The young ruler liked to drive a two-horse __Kingdom__.

7. Modern Egypt is quite different from __tomb__ Egypt.

8. An announcement praised Tutankhamen for all he did to help the __chariot__.

9. After three thousand years, Howard Carter found the boy king's __throne__.

Writing: Capitalization

Use with student text page 386.

Capitalize Titles and Punctuate Possessive Nouns

A **title** is a name given to a person or to a family as a sign of honor or respect. A title may also show a person's rank or profession. A title is capitalized when used before a person's name.

<u>King</u> Akhenaten   <u>Queen</u> Nefertiti   <u>Professor</u> Howard Carter

A **possessive noun** shows ownership. Add an apostrophe (') and an *s* after a singular noun to show possession. A singular noun refers to just one thing.

Eventually Tutankhamen**'s** brother Akhenaten died.

A. ➤ Rewrite each sentence by capitalizing titles correctly.

1. Most historians think Tutankhamen was the brother of king Akhenaten.

_____

2. Akhenaten's wife was queen Nefertiti.

_____

3. An Englishman, professor Howard Carter, found Tutankhamen's tomb.

_____

4. Long after Tutankhamen ruled, the famous queen Cleopatra ruled Egypt.

_____

5. A present-day Englishman interested in archaeology is prince Charles.

_____

B. ➤ Edit this paragraph. Then rewrite it to correct the punctuation of possessive nouns.

Tutankhamen became his countrys ruler when he was about nine years old. The new pharaohs family was from Thebes. In Tutankhamens time, it was not unusual for a boy to claim his kingdoms throne. When Howard Carter found Tutankhamens tomb, the pharaohs name became famous. Even by todays standards the tombs treasures are among the most beautiful ever seen.

_____

_____

_____

_____

_____

Elements of Literature

Use with student text page 387.

Identify Themes Across Cultures

The **theme** is the main idea or meaning of a piece of writing. The theme is usually an idea that can be identified and understood across cultures.

➤ Read each paragraph. Decide which theme best fits the paragraph. Write the number.

Theme 1: "Some people become famous by accident or chance."

Theme 2: "Age does not limit a person's ability to do great things."

1. Tutankhaten ruled successfully for the next few years with his wife. When he was about thirteen, the temples of Egypt displayed an announcement that praised all the things he had done to help the kingdom. These announcements were carved on flat pieces of stone. When he turned sixteen, Tutankhaten was considered a man and ruled the kingdom alone.

   _____

2. More than three thousand years later, an English archaeologist named Howard Carter found Tutankhamen's tomb. It yielded some of the most beautiful Egyptian treasures ever found and made the pharaoh's name famous all over the world. Though his rule was short-lived, Tutankhamen, "the boy king," will never be forgotten because of the riches he left behind.

   _____

Name _____ Date _____

Word Study

Use with student text page 388.

Recognize the Suffix *–ian*

A **suffix** is a group of letters added to the end of a word. The suffix *–ian* is a common suffix that means "a person who works with or studies something." When the suffix is added to a word like *library,* it becomes *librarian,* or someone who "works at the library."

A. ➤ Match the word to its definition. The root of each word will help you find its definition.

Word Ending in *–ian*

1. _____ mathematician
2. _____ electrician
3. _____ historian
4. _____ statistician
5. _____ technician
6. _____ grammarian

Definition

a. a person who works with or uses technical things

b. a person who knows a lot about history

c. a person who knows a lot about mathematics

d. a person who works with electricity

e. a person who knows a lot about the grammar of a language

f. a person who knows a lot about statistics or facts about numbers

B. ➤ In each sentence, find the word that ends with *–ian* and underline it. Then write a new sentence using the word. Use a dictionary.

1. A <u>statistician</u> made a graph of all the numbers we gave him.

   A statistician knows a lot about numbers.

2. The school hired a dietitian to help plan healthy meals.

   _____

3. An electrician must handle wires very carefully.

   _____

4. The writer asked a grammarian to edit her book.

   _____

Grammar Focus

Use with student text page 388.

Understand and Use Modal Auxiliaries

The words *would* and *might* are **modal auxiliaries.** They are helping verbs that are used with other verbs. *Would* and *might* are often used to express that something in the past was possible or very likely.

His education <u>would</u> have included mathematics.

He <u>might</u> have played a game like checkers.

Sentence Beginning	Verb Phrase			Sentence Ending
	Model Auxiliary	Have	Past Participle	
His education	would	have	included	mathematics.
Tutankhamon	would	have	used	papyrus to write on.
Sometimes he	might	have	hunted	animals.

A. ➤ Underline the modal auxiliary in each sentence. Then write the entire verb phrase.

1. Tutankhamen <u>might</u> have enjoyed walking in the palace gardens.

   Verb phrase: _might have enjoyed_

2. The boy might have lived with King Akhenaten and Queen Nefertiti.

   Verb phrase: _____

3. His tutor would have marked his errors in red ink.

   Verb phrase: _____

4. Tutankhamen would have learned to shoot a bow and arrow.

   Verb phrase: _____

B. ➤ Write sentences using modal auxiliaries. Look at the chart for help.

1. _____

2. _____

3. _____

Grammar Focus

Use with student text page 388.

Use Modal Auxiliaries

The **modal auxiliary** verbs *would* and *might* have different meanings. *Would* can suggests "intention or something is almost certainly true." *Might* suggests that "possibility."

The word you choose will depend on what meaning you want your sentence to have. Compare the meanings of the two sentences in this chart:

Sentence	Meaning
The dog <u>would</u> have barked.	I'm almost certain.
The dog <u>might</u> have barked.	It is possible, but I'm not sure.

A. ➤ Complete the sentences with *would* or *might*. Choose the word that matches the definition after each sentence.

1. The boy king ___*would*___ have started school at about age four. (almost certainly)

2. He also _____ have learned to wrestle and swim. (almost certainly)

3. Indoors, he _____ have played a game called *senet*. (possibly)

4. Tutankhamen _____ have injured his head in battle. (possibly)

5. Scholars think it is unlikely he _____ have recovered. (almost certainly)

6. The pharaoh _____ have lived to old age if he had not been injured. (possibly)

7. The palace guards _____ have attempted to protect him. (almost certainly)

8. If he had lived, he _____ have ruled for many years. (almost certainly)

B. ➤ Write sentences using *would* and *might* to express ideas that happened in the past.

1. _____

2. _____

3. _____

4. _____

Student Handbook

From Reading to Writing

Use with student text page 389.

Edit a Biography

➤ Directions: Use the checklist to edit the biography you wrote in Chapter 3.

Editing Checklist for a Biography

Title of biography: _____

What I did:

_____ **1.** I interviewed a friend to find out about his or her life.

_____ **2.** I took notes during the interview.

_____ **3.** I combined some sentences to form compounds with *and* or *but*.

_____ **4.** I formed some complex sentences with *because, if,* or *when*.

_____ **5.** I used transition words such as *then, next,* or *finally*.

_____ **6.** I organized my biography into three paragraphs.

_____ **7.** I gave my friend's name, birth date, address, and school.

Across Content Areas

Use with student text page 389.

Use a Map

This map of Africa is an outline map. It shows the boundaries of countries. Some of the countries are labeled. It also shows main bodies of water, such as oceans or seas.

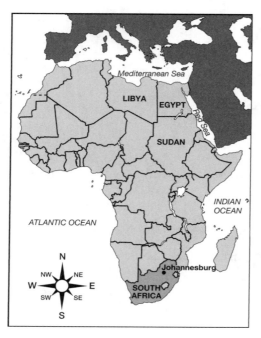

➤ Use the map to underline the correct word in each sentence.

1. Africa is a **country/<u>continent</u>.**

2. The body of water to the east of Egypt is the **Red Sea/Mediterranean Sea.**

3. The body of water to the north of Egypt is the **Red Sea/Mediterranean Sea.**

4. The country Sudan is to the **east/south** of Egypt.

5. **Libya/Sudan** is to the west of Egypt.

6. The body of water to the **east/west** of Africa is the Indian Ocean.

7. The **Atlantic Ocean/Mediterranean Sea** is to the west of Africa.

8. The largest body of water that borders Egypt is the **Red Sea/Mediterranean Sea.**

Build Vocabulary

Use with student text page 391.

Learn Multiple Meaning Words

English has many words that have more than one meaning. Some words have several meanings.

➤ Read the words and definitions. Match the underlined word in each sentence to its correct meaning. The first one has been done for you.

box	**a.** a square or rectangular container
	b. to fight with the fists
hand	**a.** the body part attached to the arm
	b. to give, to deliver
roll	**a.** to move on wheels
	b. a small, round piece of bread
fly	**a.** to move through the air
	b. an insect
sound	**a.** a noise
	b. reasonable or sensible
story	**a.** events written down or told
	b. one level of a building
palm	**a.** a tree that grows in warm climates
	b. the inner part of the hand
draw	**a.** to make lines with a pencil or pen
	b. to pull apart or pull together

1. ___*a*___ A robot's <u>hand</u> can grab tiny objects.

2. _____ You can communicate by forming letters in a person's <u>palm</u>.

3. _____ Some robot planes <u>fly</u> into dangerous storms.

4. _____ The robot is programmed to make <u>rolls</u> for the bakery.

5. _____ An elevator lifts her wheelchair from one <u>story</u> to another.

6. _____ Some robots look like a <u>box</u> on wheels.

7. _____ The disabled teen uses a robot arm to <u>draw</u> his curtains.

8. _____ A robot guided by <u>sound</u> helps people with disabilities.

Writing: Spelling

Use with student text page 400.

Spell Plurals of Regular Nouns

A **noun** names a person, place, or thing. Most nouns form **plurals** by adding –s to the end of the word.

job + s = <u>jobs</u>   hand + s = <u>hands</u>

letter + s = <u>letters</u>   problem + s = <u>problems</u>

Some nouns form their plurals in other ways, such as words that end in a consonant + *y*. To form the plural, change the *y* to *i* and add –*es*.

activity = activit**ies**

Rule	Examples
To form the plural of most nouns, add -s.	picture–*pictures* leg–*legs* object–*objects*
To form the plural of nouns ending in a consonant + *y*, change *y* to *i* and add -es.	country–*countries* emergency–*emergencies*

A. ➤ Write each word in its plural form. Use the spelling rules in the chart to help you.

1. (robot)   Some _____ travel under water or fly through the air.

2. (engineer) The _____ in Delaware have developed helpful equipment.

3. (factory)   Many _____ use robots to do dangerous jobs.

4. (limb)   Some disabled people have trouble controlling their _____.

5. (disability) People with _____ are helping test new equipment.

B. ➤ Edit each sentence. Rewrite each sentence with correct plural noun forms.

1. Some robots have amazing abilitys.

_____

2. A robot might open doores for people.

_____

3. Only human beings can enjoy jokes and tell storys.

_____

Elements of Literature

Use with student text page 401.

Analyze Text Evidence

Informational texts present important ideas about things that are real. Writers use examples to support their ideas. These examples are called **text evidence.**

Important Idea: Robots help disabled people.

Text Evidence: A robot arm can take a book off a shelf.

A robot arm can open a door.

A. ➤ Match each important idea to the text evidence that supports the idea. Sometimes more than one answer is possible.

Important Idea

1. _____ Some robots seem to be alive.

2. _____ Robots do many of the things people do.

3. _____ Robots go places people can't go.

4. _____ Engineers are developing robots to help disabled people.

5. _____ Some robots can "see."

6. _____ Robots don't have human emotions.

7. _____ Robots do some jobs better than people.

8. _____ Robots are run by computer programs.

Text Evidence

a. Bern Gavlick is testing a robot arm attached to his wheelchair.

b. A robot might have an electronic "eye" that tells if something is in its way.

c. No one can handle very tiny objects as easily as robot fingers can.

d. If a computer program is changed, a robot's job will change.

e. Some robots go to the ocean bottom.

f. Robots can't feel happy or love someone.

g. Some robots make choices like people do.

h. Robots use tools and build things.

B. ➤ Two sentences in each group are text evidence. One sentence is the important idea. Underline the sentence that is the important idea.

1. **a.** A robot could just be a box.
   b. Most robots we have today don't look anything like people.
   c. A robot could be an arm without a body.

2. **a.** Robots can work in areas full of dangerous fumes.
   b. Robots can handle boiling liquids.
   c. Robots often do jobs that are unsafe for people.

3. **a.** One teen is testing a device attached to his wheelchair.
   b. Some disabled teens are testing new devices.
   c. One teen is testing a video game system.

Word Study

Use with student text page 402.

Learn Adverbs of Frequency

The word *frequency* means "how often something happens." **Adverbs of frequency** are words that describe how often something happens.

The chart shows the most common adverbs of frequency and their meanings.

Adverbs of Frequency	
Frequency Words	**Meaning**
never	not at any time
rarely, seldom	almost never, not often
sometimes, occasionally	from time to time, not every time
often, frequently	over and over again
always	at all times

➤ Rewrite each sentence. Replace the underlined phrase with an adverb of frequency.

1. Factories <u>over and over again</u> use robots to do dangerous jobs.

   _____

2. Robots <u>almost never</u> have legs.

   _____

3. Some teenagers are <u>not at any time</u> able to leave their wheelchairs.

   _____

4. A robot's job <u>at all times</u> depends on its computer program.

   _____

5. Robots are <u>from time to time</u> guided by sound.

   _____

VISIONS A Activity Book • Copyright © Heinle

Grammar Focus

Use with student text page 402.

Use Adverbs of Frequency

Adverbs describe verbs. **Adverbs of frequency** tell how often an action happens.

Robots *never* feel emotions.

That robot's arm *always* moves to the left.

Robots *sometimes* fly airplanes.

Adverbs of Frequency		
never	sometimes	frequently
rarely	occasionally	always
seldom	often	

A. ➤ Underline the verb in each sentence. Then choose an adverb of frequency to complete the sentence. Write it in the space.

1. In science fiction movies, you _____ see androids or human-looking robots.

2. Many disabled people have _____ used a robot arm.

3. Robots _____ do dangerous work in factories.

4. Today's robots are _____ controlled by computer programs.

5. Busy engineers _____ build robots just for fun.

6. People _____ laugh at odd-looking robots.

B. ➤ Write sentences using adverbs of frequency. Use a different adverb in each sentence.

1. _____

2. _____

3. _____

4. _____

VISIONS Unit 6 • Chapter 4 It Could Still Be a Robot

Grammar Focus

Use with student text page 402.

Use Adverbs of Frequency with *Be* and Other Verbs

In sentences with the verb *be*, the adverb of frequency comes after the verb. In sentences with other verbs, the adverb of frequency comes before the verb.

Adverbs of Frequency				
		Verb	**Adverb**	
With the Verb Be	Robots	are	sometimes	on wheels.
	A robot	is	always	ready for work.
		Adverb	**Verb**	
With Other Verbs	Robots	never	get	bored or tired.
	Krista	often	uses	finger spelling.

A. ➤ Rewrite the sentences with the adverb of frequency in the correct position. Use the chart for help.

1. (seldom)   Robots look like people.

_____

2. (never)   They are really human beings.

_____

3. (often)   Robots help people with disabilities.

_____

4. (always)   The students are excited about the new devices.

_____

5. (sometimes)   A robot arm is on the side of a wheelchair.

_____

6. (frequently)   Robots do jobs faster than human beings.

_____

Student Handbook

From Reading to Writing

Use with student text page 403.

Edit a Persuasive Essay

➤ Use the checklist to edit the persuasive essay you wrote in Chapter 4.

Editing Checklist for a Persuasive Essay

Title of essay: _____

What I did:

_____ 1. I explained why people should use robots.

_____ 2. I wrote three paragraphs—introduction, body, and conclusion.

_____ 3. I told what my essay was about in the first paragraph.

_____ 4. I included my thesis statement in the first paragraph.

_____ 5. I gave details supporting my thesis statement in the second paragraph.

_____ 6. I included examples in the second paragraph.

_____ 7. I restated my thesis statement in the third paragraph.

_____ 8. I convinced my readers to agree with my ideas.

VISIONS **Unit 6 • Chapter 4** It Could Still Be a Robot

Across Content Areas

Use with student text page 403.

Compare and Contrast Texts

When you **compare and contrast,** you examine the similarities and differences of two things.

A. ➤ Read the informational paragraphs about robots. Use the Venn diagram to **compare and contrast** people and robots.

Robots are not alive. They are machines run by computers. A robot may be an arm without a body. It may be just a box. A robot may move around, but walking on two legs is hard for it.

Robots can handle very tiny objects better than people. They can go places where people can't go, such as the ocean bottom or the planet Mars. Like people, robots can solve math problems, draw pictures, and play a musical instrument. Like people, they can help those with disabilities. But robots cannot enjoy a joke, taste food, or love someone. After all, they are machines, not people.

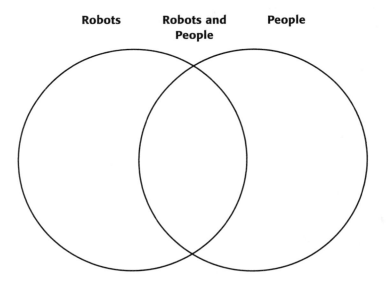

Robots   **Robots and People**   **People**

B. ➤ Write a paragraph describing how robots and people are the same and how they are different.

_____

_____

_____

_____